REMARKABLE
REBIRTH

REMARKABLE REBIRTH

The Early History of the Armenians in Detroit

Dr. Ashod Rhaffi Aprahamian

Cover design by Andrew Mehall
Page design by Sans Serif, Inc.

Printed in the United States

CONTENTS

PREFACE

Reading this densely documented historical volume, the reader would wonder why a person, destined to become a medical doctor, would go to such lengths to reconstruct the Armenian community life in his hometown of Detroit. The answer perhaps lies in the fact that Ashod Rhaffi Aprahamian comes from a clan deeply affected by history and conditioned to view life from a historic perspective. He is also endowed with an atavistic impulse to record life for posterity, as other members of his family have done, out of a deep commitment to their ancestral heritage.

This book, originally entitled *The Armenians in Detroit,* is a labor of love and an expression of devotion to reconstruct the fabric of traditional life in a city and community that had to play a pivotal role in the development of the American-Armenian community, and, for that matter, the evolvement of Diaspora Armenian life.

This volume predates the major work on American-Armenian immigrant experience by John Mirak, who later came not only to document, but also analyze the Armenian immigrant experience in his book entitled *Torn in Between Two Lands.*

At the time Aprahamian's book was written (1957) there were very few publications about American-Armenian history, like M. V. Malcom's *The Armenians in America*, Sarkis Atarnian's *The Armenian Community,* and a few minor theses about the Armenian communities in California. In that respect, therefore, Aprahamian's book may be counted among pioneering works to document early Armenian life in America. That position is further substantiated by the fact that the book is mostly based on primary sources: personal interviews by major players in the community development, church minutes, and reports researched first-hand through archives.

Therefore, besides providing an interesting background of community development, it contains a profusion of reliable facts and documents for future historians.

Although modest in size, the book covers the entire gamut of Armenian community life in Detroit: the first cultural shock of the immigrant population, its ambivalence on continuing life in the new world or returning to the old country, the burgeoning life around social and political clubs, involvement in commercial activities, development of religious, charitable and educational institutions, etc., all within the context of broader Armenian experience throughout the U.S. and in comparison with other ethnic groups. Detroit was, in a way, the microcosm of the cauldron name "the melting pot."

While describing and analyzing the functions of different groups, the author has bent backwards to research the root causes of community problems and present community structure in its present state.

One important fact, which is missed by many Armenians in America, the split in the Armenian Apostolic Church in America since 1933, has been thoroughly investigated and capsulized for the reader to grasp the background of the divisions in the community. And that is done with the honest objectivity of a historian, albeit leaving no doubt as to the author's sympathies and affiliations.

The reader is left in awe reading about the tremendous body of research to come up with this concise volume, which indicates the seriousness of intent of the writer and his integrity in conducting his incisive analyses.

Had the author remained in academia, rather than shifting his pursuit to the medical field, he would certainly have continued the line of history, whose foundations he has anchored solidly in this volume, and come up with a comprehensive book covering most recent history. Perhaps that has to be left to younger scholars to complement the present work.

Reading this book, many Detroit Armenians will discover their own family history, as the historians weaving a broader picture of Armenian immigrant experience will encounter a valuable stone to complement the mosaic of American-Armenian history.

As the book is published posthumously, it also represents a tribute to the memory of a person who nurtured deep interest and love to the Armenian past and who faced its future with trepidation.

Edmond Y. Azadian
Author, Journalist and Family Friend

Ashod Rhaffi Remembered

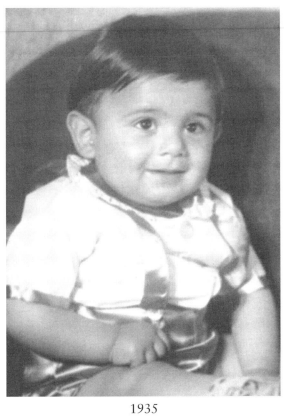

1935

1948

High School Graduation. June 1952

1980

ACKNOWLEDGEMENT

I wish to record my gratitude to all those persons who have made the writing of this thesis possible.

Thanks go to the staffs of the Burton Historical Collection of the Detroit Public Library and the Social Studies division of the Wayne State University Library for their assistance.

A great debt of gratitude is owed to all those persons, too numerous to mention here, who so graciously consented to being interviewed. Much of the content of this thesis is based upon the information gained from these interviews.

I especially wish to thank the following people: The Rev. Arnak Kasparian, The Rev. Diran Papazian, and Mr. Archie Yeghissian, chairman of the St. John Armenian Church Parish Council, for their cooperation in allowing access to the church records; Mr. Souren Aprahamian, my father, for translating the "Minutes of the Parish Council of St. John Armenian Church" and rendering other valuable aid; Professor Joe L. Norris who originally suggested the topic; and Professor Sidney Glazer for his guidance and constructive criticism during the writing of this thesis.

Ashod Rhaffi Aprahamian

1

Introduction

ACCORDING TO TRADITION, THE FOUNDERS OF CHRISTIANITY IN Armenia were the Apostle Bartholomew and Thaddeus, one of the Seventy. The period of their work in Armenia is usually put at 35–60 A.D. It is on the basis of this tradition that ". . . the Armenian Church bases its claim to apostolicity."[1]

However, Armenia did not become Christian until the arrival of Gregory the Illuminator in the latter part of the third century. King Tiridates was converted to Christianity by Gregory, and in 301 A.D. the king issued a royal proclamation declaring Christianity the accepted state religion.[2]

One hundred fifty years later, the strength of the hold of Christianity on the Armenian people was severely tested as the Sassanid Kings of Persia determined to consolidate a united front against the Roman Empire by spreading the Mazdean religion throughout

Armenia.[3] Vartan Mamikonian (now St. Vartan), then a famous soldier, was among the Armenian delegates who went to plead with King Yezdedjerd II to rescind his decree against Christianity.[4] The pleas were in vain and the Armenians decided to fight.

They raised a volunteer army of 66,000 under the leadership of Vartan; the Armenian army met the Persian army of 300,000 men on the plain of Avaryr, south of Mt. Ararat. The Armenians were defeated as Vartan and 1,035 fellow martyrs fell.[5] However, the ferocity of the resistance put up by the Armenians and the danger posed by the Huns to the borders of Persia caused the Persians to abandon their efforts to convert the Armenians. According to Jacques De Morgan, the battle of Avaryr saved the Armenian nation.[6]

However, the tribulations of the Armenians were not over as its geographic location made it a buffer state that was yet to be crossed many times by invading armies. The Arabs and the Byzantine Empire took turns occupying Armenia, which naturally resulted in suffering and brutality.[7] This continual state of unrest caused some of the Armenians to leave their homeland. In the eleventh century, after periodic invasions by the Seljuk, a large group of Armenians—20,000 to 50,000—migrated to Poland. By the fourteenth century, additional migrations had raised the number of Armenians in Poland to 200,000.

Other groups of Armenians went to Transylvania, Moldavia, and the Crimea. In 1375 the last king of Armenia Minor (located in Cilicia) ". . . was carried away by the fierce Mamelukes of Egypt." The emigration continued as groups of Armenians went to Wallachia and the surrounding lands south of the Danube; to Persia; to south central Asia, including "Calcutta, Madras, Bombay, Batavia, and other places."[8] Thus it is seen that the Armenian people have been emigrating from their homeland for centuries.

The Armenian people, both in and out of their historic homeland, have been held together by the Armenian Church. Today the Armenian Church is still important in the lives of Armenians throughout the world. This role of the church, as well as some background on the church, will be discussed later in this paper.

The first Armenian to land in America was a member of the Jamestown Colony known as John the Armenian who landed in 1618 or 1619.[9] However, John the Armenian did not start any flood of Armenians to this country. The number of Armenians who had immigrated to America by 1894 numbered only 3,000. In 1895, however, the Turks commenced another of their bloody massacres of the Armenian population. As a result many Armenians fled their homeland to find a haven from the Turks and the marauding Kurds. In the next three years slightly under 15,000 Armenians immigrated to America.

The flow of Armenians remained comparatively heavy as the tensions leading to World War I mounted and were finally loosened. From 1898 to 1917, another 55,000 Armenians came to this country. World War I saw over a million and a half Armenians killed or displaced as a result of the Turkish policy of extermination of the Armenians.

As soon as the war was over, there was another stream of Armenian immigrants coming to the United States to find peace and safety. This stream of immigrants was only cut off by the enactment of the quota system.[10] The 1930 *Census* lists 51,741 foreign born Armenian stock in the United States by mother tongue.[11] This lower figure has several explanations: this is a figure taken from the *Census* while the other figures were on immigration; many Armenians, having emigrated previous to World War I, went back to the mother country; some Turkish Armenians did not know Armenian; and finally, the last explanation, death.

The first Armenians to come to America at first settled on the east coast. However, as more came to this country, the Armenians started to go to other parts of the United States, especially into the East North Central States and California. The 1910 *Census* listed 30,021 Armenians in the United States by mother tongue, 23,938 of them foreign born.[12] In 1910 the foreign born Armenians were distributed in the following way: 10,620 in the New England States: 6,086 in the Middle Atlantic States; 2,657 in the East North Central States; and 3,179 in the Pacific States (almost all in California).

By 1920 the *Census* figures for the foreign born ran as follows: New England States, 12,459; Middle Atlantic States, 10,908; East North Central States, 6,276; and Pacific States, 6,388. In 1930 the figures for the foreign born were: New England States 16,056; Middle Atlantic States, 15,156; East North Central States, 9,949; and Pacific States, 9,239.[13]

The latest available study of the Armenian Population, *The Armenians of the United States and Canada*, gives the following figures as of 1947: New England States, 64,000; Middle Atlantic States, 64,000; East North Central States, 34,500; and Pacific States, 44,600. The total given for the whole United States is 215,000.[14] If these figures seem somewhat large compared to the *Census* figures, it must be remembered that most of the figures were for foreign born, and Armenians are not noted for small families.

Michigan did not always have the largest Armenian population of any of the East North Central States. In 1910 Illinois had a larger number of foreign born Armenians, 1,402 vs. 472. By 1920 Michigan had surpassed Illinois in the number of foreign born Armenians with 2,606 vs. 1,742 for Illinois. In 1930 Michigan had 5,434 Armenians of foreign birth compared to 2,499 in Illinois.[15] Mr. Tashjian estimated the number of Armenians in Michigan at 24,000 in 1947. Thus ranking it behind California with 43,500, New York with 40,000 and Massachusetts with 35,000, as the states with the largest number of inhabitants of Armenian descent.

The Detroit Metropolitan area contains most of the Armenians in Michigan, and would rank behind New York, Los Angeles, and Boston Metropolitan areas in the number of Armenians.[16]

2

Population, Early History, and Mode of Living in Detroit

CCORDING TO AN ARTICLE WRITTEN FOR A ST. JOHN Armenian Church publication of 1931, the first Armenian in Detroit was an Esther Nevart. She was brought to Detroit by Armenian missionaries (no date given) and raised in the city. Esther Nevart became a doctor and later married a non-Armenian.[1] The story of Esther Nevart closely resembles the story of Nectar M. Kalaijian, who was, according to a *Detroit News* article of September 6, 1896, the first Armenian in Detroit, Nectar was brought to Detroit from Armenia by missionaries and "placed in the charge of the people of Plum Street Christian Church." She attended public school in Detroit, then went to Kentucky to go to high school. Returning from Kentucky, she entered the Michigan College of Medicine and Surgery.

Nectar Kalaijian became the first Armenian woman physician in Michigan. Dr. Kalaijian set up practice in Detroit in an office on Sixth Street in 1895.[2] In 1898 she married Howard Fisk of Detroit.[3]

Because of the resemblance of the two stories and because the church publication article was based in the memories of long time Detroit residents, it seems evident the Esther Nevart and Nectar Kalaijian are one and the same person, and that the article in the church publication supplies the wrong name.[4] The article in the *Detroit News* of 1896 puts the number of Armenian in Detroit at ". . . about a dozen." The same article also relates that ". . . the only Armenian baby born in Detroit is little Lavon Jambarjian. He is nine months old and lives with his parents on Sixth Street."[5]

Although the date of the arrival of the first Armenian in Detroit is unknown, by 1900 there were fifty-four Armenians in the city.[6] The 1910 Census shows that there were 338 Armenians in Detroit, with 317 of these being of foreign birth.[7] There was a considerable increase in the number of Armenians in 1920 as the Census showed 1,692 Armenian speaking people of whom 1,422 were foreign born.[8] The largest increase in the number of Armenians took place in the early 1920's as many Armenian men brought their families and/or women to marry, to Detroit. The 1930 Census listed 2,247 Armenian foreign born by country of birth, in Detroit. Another 442 were listed in Highland Park.[9] Native born Armenians of foreign or mixed parentage by country of birth for Detroit and Highland Park were 1,356 and 326 respectively.[10] Today estimates of Metropolitan Detroit's Armenian population range from 16,000 to 25,000 people.[11]

World War I saw the massacre and displacement of one and a half million Armenians. This convinced any of the Armenians of the city who ever had any intentions of returning to their homeland that such would be impossible. These people, like the other Armenians of Detroit, now went about trying to build new lives in America.[12]

The policy of extermination of the Armenians adopted by the Turks, plus the " natural" hatred of Turkey in the minds of thousand of Armenians in the United States, caused them to fight against their hated enemy. Many young Armenian men from Detroit joined a volunteer regiment of Armenians from the United States to fight the Turks. By 1915 8,000 Armenians were with Allenby's army fighting in Palestine.[13]

The Armenians who came to America after World War I had suffered long and hard. The horrors they suffered made them hate Turkey even to the present day.

Aside from the above mentioned articles on Dr. Kalaijian, there is no information available on the Armenians who came to Detroit before the turn of the century. However, with the help of Armenians who have resided in Detroit for forty or fifty years, it is possible to obtain a picture of the life of the Armenian community in Detroit in the first years of this century.

The Armenians who came to Detroit in the early years of the century scattered throughout the city. However, by 1907 at least, many Armenians started settling in the West Jefferson and South Solvay area of Delray. The Armenian community of Detroit was almost wholly populated with young males. These young Armenian immigrants came to the United States either to escape the tyranny and brutality of the Turks or to earn money to take back to Armenia in order to improve their economic status in their homeland.

Because of their motives in coming to Detroit for only a short time before going back home and because of the shortage of Armenian woman which was to last for a number of years, these men lived as bachelors.[14] The men either lived in boarding houses or, more commonly, a group of ten to fifteen men from the same village or region of Armenia would get together and rent a house. One person would do all the housework and cooking while the others worked.[15]

These people were preponderantly of peasant background. They had little knowledge of the English language and what leisure time they had, they spent among themselves.

The only social outlets at the time were the political parties (see Chapter 8) and the one Armenian coffee house then operating in Detroit. At that early date (before 1908) two of the political parties had organizations in Detroit. The Dashnaktzoutyoun or Armenian Revolutionary Federation organized its Detroit branch in 1904.[16] The Hunchak party's Detroit chapter was organized three years later, in 1907. The men would sit in the coffee house or in the rented political clubroom and talk politics for hours on end. The independence of Turkish Armenia continued to be the most important topic of conversation among Detroit Armenians for a number of years.[17]

The year 1908 saw the start of a new influx of Armenians to the United States and, consequently, to Detroit. In that year a new law went into effect in the Ottoman Empire subjecting Armenians to service in the Turkish Army.[18] Though many Armenians came to the United States to escape service in the Turkish Army, there were still quite a few who came to this country in order to make money to take back to the homeland. The Armenian immigrants coming to Detroit remained overwhelmingly of peasant origin though a few city bred Armenians could be found among them.[19]

With this influx of Armenians, the number of Armenian coffee houses and restaurants increased and the Delray Armenian community, still isolated from the rest of the city because of the language barrier, began to take on a different atmosphere. The growing community, still preponderantly made up of single young men,[20] became less sedate. Some of the coffee houses became places for gambling and drinking of alcoholic beverages, as well as the usual card games and backgammon.[21]

The wave of Armenians who came to Detroit after 1908 came

here primarily to find a job. About the only other motive in coming to the city was to be near a relative. Though some Armenians had been able to bring some of their wealth from the homeland to America, most of them landed in this country with little money. In most cases those who came to Detroit did not come to the city immediately after landing. Some stayed in eastern cities such as Boston, Providence, or New York for months before coming to Detroit in hopes of earning more money. Others traveled to many parts of the country in their search for a job before finally coming to Detroit after many months of wandering.

As these men, of varying economic status, came to Detroit, the manner of living in the Armenian community began to change. No longer was it usual for the men to gather into groups to set up housekeeping. It became the usual practice to rent or board. The restaurants and coffee houses had upstairs rooms for rent. Other Armenians began buying some homes in the area of Solvay and West Jefferson which at that time were selling for from $1,500 to $2,000 and, since they were single, turning the homes into boarding houses.[22] Though there were few Armenian married couples in the city before World War I—all estimates place the number at considerably less than thirty—some of them also took in boarders. Room and board costs ranged from $2.00 to $3.50 per week in all these places.[23] Some of the rooms above the restaurants, coffee houses, and some of the rooming houses were almost unfit for human habitation. There were two or three beds to a small room, bed bugs were plentiful and in the summer there were insects as screens on any windows were a rarity.[24]

Whatever may be said about some of the rooms, the food prepared in the Armenian restaurants was always considered to be from fairly good to excellent. Armenian food was always served. Pilaf (rice cooked in chicken broth) Persian style (with raisins) was served almost every day with a variety of other Armenian foods. One of the Armenian restaurants in Delray had as a part owner a famous Armenian chef from Constantinople. He kept his reputation as a fine cook while in Detroit.[25]

After World War I, as the last wave of Armenian immigrants swelled Detroit's Armenian population, the number of Armenians in Delray on South Solvay, West Jefferson, Greene, Cotterall, Harrington, and Post increased. Though the Armenian Delray community had been quite lively before the war with the coffee houses and other Armenian businesses established, now, as the population had boomed, so did the number of Armenian owned business establishments especially on the first two blocks of South Solvay going north from Jefferson.

At its height, in the 1920's, the area had about ten coffee houses, and at least as many restaurants. There were also numerous other business establishments including grocery stores, barber shops, shoe repair shops, dry goods stores, and confectionery shops. South Solvay, as the center of the community, came to be associated with the Armenians and, beginning even before the decade of the twenties, the street car conductors on West Jefferson would call out "Armenian boulevard" for the South Solvay stop.[26] South Solvay was a "live" street and if something unusual happened, such as a fight or an accident, hundreds of men would pour out from the restaurants and coffee houses to find out what was happening.[27] At its height, in the late 1930's, the Delray Armenian community must have been numbered about 2,000 or more.[28]

The depression hit the Delray Armenian community hard. However, the people of the community cooperated as best they could to help their fellow Armenians who were in need. Armenian grocers, restaurant owners, and other Armenian businessmen gave credit rather than have their fellow Armenians suffer. One Armenian restaurant, owned by three partners, averaged seventy-five cents profit a week for long stretches as the owners extended thousands of dollars of credit.[29]

As a result of extending credit, some Armenian businessmen went bankrupt. Though some Armenians did go on the public relief, it is believed that the percentage of Armenians on relief was much less than the percentage of the entire city population on relief. This belief is supported in a study made by R. T. La Piere on the Fresno Armenians. Mr. La Piere found that the County Welfare Bureau in the 1930's handled about one application for charity per year for each five hundred Armenians in the country. For the entire population the rate was ". . . one for each 100." Mr. La Piere wrote: . . . that the Armenians were ashamed to demand public charity, believing that responsibility for the indigent begins at home."[30]

As the economic situation in Detroit started to improve in the late 1930's and early 1940's, the Armenians in Delray gradually moved out. As the Armenians moved out, Negroes moved in. Today (1958) it is estimated that there are at most, one hundred Armenians in the area. Many of those Armenians who have stayed are middle-aged or beyond. There are very few young Armenians living in this area. Though the people have moved out, many of the businesses still are run by Armenians.[31]

There are presently only two coffee houses left on S. Solvay. However, one is more like a restaurant, while the other, located at 714 S. Solvay, is still a remnant of the coffee houses of thirty and forty years ago. One can walk into it today and see what occurred in a coffee-house of long ago. The only changes are that the men are older, better dressed, and there are only one or two young men in the crowd. The men come from all over the metropolitan area to sit, talk, and play cards and backgammon while sipping Turkish coffee or a soft drink.[32]

As mentioned above, all the Detroit Armenians did not settle in Delray. They scattered throughout the city as indicated by the various locations of Armenian businesses. However, the Armenians did start settling in another concentrated area because of the Ford Highland Park Plant. (Ford's announcement of the five dollar day drew many Armenians to Detroit in 1913). Armenians have been working at Ford for at least fifty years.[33] Beginning before the 1920's, Armenians began moving to Highland Park and the surrounding area to be near their work. Another reason for moving out to this area was that to some it signified a social climb.[34] In a few years, the area bounded by Brush on the east, Kendall on the north, Fourteenth Street on the west, and Cortland on the south had many Armenian families.

There were other scattered Armenians families living near the above named area. Though these Armenians were well spread out, compared to the compact Delray community, they came to supply the leadership and the financial support for the activities of the Detroit Armenian community. By the late twenties and early thirties, one could see evidence of the leadership supplied by the Armenians of this area in and around Highland Park. The two strong political parties, the A. R. F. and the Armenian Democratic Liberal Party, had club-houses in Highland Park on Grand Avenue and Woodward respectively. The site of St. John Armenian Church was selected in order to be near this "concentration" of Armenians.[35] This is to be contrasted with the failure of the Delray community to support church services in Delray in the early thirties.

Though the Armenians in the area of Highland Park had more drive, seemed more anxious to better themselves, and supplied the community leaders (in the sense that the community leaders moved to this area), they never developed a community quite like the Delray Armenian community. Only two Armenian coffee houses were located in this area, on Hamilton near Labelle, and on Woodrow Wilson, between Ford and Pasadena. There were, however, many Armenian owned businesses of various types including two groceries specializing in imported foods.

One of the important reasons for this difference between the two communities was that the Armenians in and around Highland Park were, when compared to the Armenian population of Delray, widely scattered. Another, and perhaps the more important reason, was that there were more family men in Highland Park. These men, with their homes, families, and jobs, were not interested in gathering at coffee houses and restaurants.

Today many Armenians have left the Highland Park area and have scattered into northwest Detroit and the suburbs in that direction. There are, however, between one and two thousand Armenians still residing in the area.[36] There is only one other area in Detroit that has a large Armenian population. Armenians in the 1920's and 1930's began moving west and north out of Delray, still staying in southwest Detroit. The Armenian Revolutionary Federation's Armenian Community Center and the St. Sarkis Armenian Church (see Chapter 8) are in this Lafayette, Waterman area.

The last large group of Armenians to come to Detroit came in the years following World War II when about 600 of 3,000 Armenian refugees entering the United States came to Detroit.[37] These displaced persons were brought to the United States by the Armenian National Committee to Aid Homeless Armenians. This organization was founded by George Mardigian, the proprietor of the Omar Khayyam Restaurant in San Francisco.[38]

In 1945 the Soviet Armenian government started a program for the resettlement of refugee Armenians. More than 100,000 Armenians were resettled in Soviet Armenia under this program. The Armenians were mainly refugees from Europe and the Middle East, but 350 Armenians holding American citizenship went to Armenia under this program.[39] Under this program twenty-seven Armenians from Detroit went to the Soviet Union in 1947. They were followed by thirty-four more Armenians in 1949. The people who left Detroit were mostly older people, forty to seventy years of age. Many of them had close relatives in Armenia and had little in the way of relatives to hold them in this country. There were only three or four families in the sixty-one Detroit people who returned to Armenia.[40]

3

Commercial Life

THE ARMENIANS WHO CAME TO THE UNITED STATES, AS had other Armenians who had emigrated from their historic homeland, tended to settle in urban areas.[1] This is especially true of Michigan Armenians who settled in the urban areas of Detroit, Flint, and Grand Rapids. The people quickly entered the commercial life of the area. Since many came to the United States only with the idea of making some money, then returning to Armenia, working in a factory suited their ends. Others, who came with the intention of staying in the United States, also found work in factories either because they had no trade, coming from a peasant background, or because they did not have the capital to start a business of their own.

It is safe to say that most of the Armenians of Detroit before World War I were factory workers. Many of the Armenians found jobs at the factories in and around Delray. Some of these factories were German Brass (later changed to Michigan Brass), Solvay, Solvay Process, Michigan Malleable Iron, and Michigan Marble.[2] There were also many Armenians employed in the various automobile factories, especially Ford. After Ford announced his $5.00 a day wage, a Ford factory badge became something to be worn proudly among some Armenians. This can be readily understood when it is remembered that the usual rate of pay before World War I was ten to fifteen cents an hour for twelve hours of work a day.[3]

Prosperity finally came to the Armenian community with the start of the war. Until this came about, many Armenians had difficulties finding a job, and once they found it, it was difficult to hold onto the job. For this reason many of the men held four, five or six or more jobs at as many different factories in the period of a few years. The comparative prosperity of the war years enabled many to save enough money to bring across to the United States their wives and families, and in some cases single men paid for the passage of their future wives.

The money earned during the war years also gave many of those who desired it enough capital to start a business of their own.[4] Though many did leave the factories to go into business, many more stayed at their jobs in various factories in and around the city. Though no survey was taken, from living in this community and from the knowledge and impressions gained from the interviews necessary to gather information, it is safe to say that the immigrant Armenians who continued working in the factories are, or were, in a fairly comfortable financial situation. They not only invested their savings in a home but also in income bearing properties such as commercial buildings, flats, apartments, and parking lots near various factory locations. An indication of this is the fact that the largest property owner among the Armenians who own property in Delray is a recently retired factory worker.[5]

The Armenians have always been noted for their success in commercial ventures. Despite the first World War and the brutality and oppression of the Turks, past and present, some of the Armenians in the cities of Turkey are still prospering in commercial enterprise, though not as well as they did before, especially prior to World War I.

The desire to go into trade was also in the Armenians who came to Detroit. Among the first commercial enterprises entered into by the Detroit Armenians were rug retailing, restaurants, coffee houses, shoe repair, and hotels.

"One of the major Armenian contributions to American commerce is the introduction of Oriental rugs. Armenian rug merchants have found their way into every important city in the Commonwealth."[6] What was written of the Armenians of Massachusetts could also be applied to Detroit Armenians. Of the twelve rug manufactures and dealers listed in the 1909 *Michigan Gazetter*, four were Armenian.[7]

Armenian owned restaurants and coffee houses were opened for business in the first years of the century to serve the Armenian community that grew in Delray. Later, as the Armenians moved into the Oakman, Hamilton, Woodward area in and around Highland Park, Armenian restaurants and coffee houses, in lesser number, were also opened in this area. Armenian owned restaurants were not opened only in areas populated by Armenians, as Armenians opened establishments all over the city, especially on the west side. Also, because a restaurant was owned by an Armenian, it did not necessarily follow that he served Armenian style cooking. Another kind of business entered into by Armenians in this area were stalls or stands on Manchester Avenue, across from Ford's Highland Park plant, to supply the wants and needs of the factory workers. At the height of activity of the plant, five of the stalls or shops catering to the workers were owned and operated by Armenians.[8]

Armenians started going into the shoe repair business almost as soon as they arrived in Detroit. They continued going into the business in the teens and the twenties. The number or proportion of Armenians going into this occupation is about the easiest to ascertain from city directories because names of the owners were listed in almost every case, instead of the name of the shop. By 1921, of about 600 shoe repair shops listed, almost sixty[9] or one out of ten were run by Armenians.[10] By 1929, of the approximately 925 shops listed, about 140 were Armenian owned, or one out of every 6.7.[11] In 1940 the proportion went even higher as 150 out of 950 establishments, or one out of 6.3 shops was run by an Armenian.[12] These are interesting figures when it is remembered that the Armenians constituted about one per cent or less of Detroit's population.

Today the number or proportion of Armenians in the shoe repair business has probably dropped, although, it is impossible to corroborate this by the use of the *City Directory* because so many shoe repair shops have the businesses' name and not the owner's name listed. Many of the Armenians probably went into the business with little or no experience and little capital.[13] Armenians went into the shoe repair business probably because it was relatively easy to learn the trade and because only a limited command of English was necessary in this business. Another motive, probably as important as the two stated above, was the desire to be one's own boss and not have the uncertainties of a factory job.[14]

After World War I, and especially in the 1920's, Armenians started to go into the grocery business in increasing numbers as war time prosperity allowed them to accumulate the necessary capital to go into business, if not alone, then with one or two partners.[15] This movement into the grocery business probably reached its height just after World War II as some returning servicemen went into it while the foreign born generation was still active enough to engage in business. There must have been about one hundred Armenians in the grocery business in the peak period.[16] The number of Armenians in this trade is greatly reduced now because of retirement and death among the foreign born, the advent of killing competition by the super markets, and the reluctance of first generation American born Armenians to continue in this line of work which entails long hours, hard work, and low profit margins.

Starting in the 1920's and continuing even today, although at a reduced rate, Armenians in considerable number have been going into the dry cleaning business. Here again is a small, one man or one family enterprise that needs, at most, only a few hired help. There are one hundred or more Armenian run dry cleaning establishments in the city.[17] Although some Armenians had a chain of three or more outlets to feed a cleaning plant, this is no longer true as almost every Armenian owned cleaning establishment is just one plant and store combined, with no other outlets. This situation has developed because the small modern cleaning machines now available enable a small store, with its own cleaning plant, to compete in price with any chain.[18] There is a totally different situation in Philadelphia where two of the city's largest dry cleaning chains are owned by Armenians.[19]

Another field of commercial enterprise that has a fairly large number of Armenians is hotels and lodging. There are between twenty and thirty Armenians in this field. They own and run every kind of lodging house from a first rate hotel to a "flop house." These hotel owners were among the first Armenians to accumulate comparatively large amounts of wealth.[20] Many of these men are active supporters of St. John Armenian Church and the Armenian General

Benevolent Union, an international charitable organization. (See Chapters 8 and 5).

In the 1930's a small number of Armenians went into small parts manufacturers or into the tool and die shop business. As the nation began to prosper in the late thirties and early forties, so did some of these men. Several of them now own factories that employ as many as 700 people. These owners are the wealthiest of the Detroit Armenians.[21]

The number of Armenians in the professions was exceeding small in the first two or three decades of the century. There were three doctors of medicine, two or three dentists, and the same number of lawyers. These men who were the early professionals usually had their pre-professional education in Armenia at one of the colleges established by Armenian Protestant Missionaries. They then came to the United States and received their professional training.[22]

However, as the Armenians improved their economic status, and as those who immigrated here as children and as the first generation Americans became adults, the situation improved considerably. At present, it is estimated that there are at least forty doctors and dentists and about thirty lawyers of Armenian descent in Detroit. There are also comparatively large numbers of Armenians in other professions, especially in engineering and education.[23]

Not all Armenians are in business or in the professions. There are still many white and blue-collar workers. Many of those who work in factories are in skilled or in semi-skilled jobs.

All these people have contributed to the economic rise by the Detroit Armenians. This economic rise by Detroit Armenians is only typical of the economic rise of Armenian communities in other cities of the United States. The Yankee City Series confirms the rise of the Armenians.

By 1933 the eight ethnic groups are arranged along the Yankee City occupational scale, by index number, in the following ascending order: Russians, 1.95: Poles, 1.97: French Canadians, 2.24; Italians, 2.28; Greeks, 2.34; Irish, 2.52; Armenians, 2.56; and Jews, 3.32. The index for total ethnics is 2.42; for total natives, 2.56.

The occupational status index applied above is nothing more than a device for stating in a convenient form the *average* rating of the occupational status of a group in terms of its aggregate advance from the base of the lowest occupational class.[24]

The authors of *The Social Systems of the American Ethnic Groups* partially ascribe this rise or increased mobility to ". . . a religious affinity between the Armenian Apostolic Church and the Episcopal Church, which led to affiliation between the two and a more rapid acculturation of the Armenian groups," and to the desire of Armenians to establish themselves permanently in this country.[25]

4

Social Life

THE SOCIAL LIFE OF THE ARMENIANS IN DETROIT BEFORE the first world war was severely limited by the language barrier and the absence of women. The only social gathering places for the Armenian community were the political clubhouses and the coffee houses.

The political parties performed more than their overt functions; they also played a vital role in the social life of the community. By the time of World War I there were four political clubs organized in Detroit. Besides the Dashnags and Hunchaks, there were Ramgavars organized in January of 1911 and the Veragazmial Hunchaks. The Ramgavars and the Veragazmials united in 1921 to form the Armenian Democratic Liberal Party.[1] The political functions of the various clubs are discussed in Chapter 8 of this paper.

The Dashnags had a clubhouse almost from the time they

organized in Detroit. They rented various store buildings for a few years, then purchased a store building at 803 Cotterall. This in turn was sold when the A. R. F. erected the Zavarian Hall in Delray in 1928.[2] About the time of World War I, the Dashnags leased another club at 77 Victor Avenue in Highland Park. They kept the Victor Avenue location until the 1940's when they moved for a few years to a building on Oakman between Twelfth Street and Woodrow Wilson. This location had to be abandoned because of the construction of the Lodge Expressway. The present day clubhouse in this section of Detroit was built on Linwood between Ford and Pasadena. It was in 1941 that the Dashnags acquired the former Masonic Temple on Lafayette and Waterman and renamed it the Armenian Community Center.[3] The Zavarian Hall in Delray was sold in 1951 because of the lack of Armenians in Delray.[4]

The Hunchaks rented a store as a clubhouse in Delray for a number of years. However, they were the weakest of the political parties and, during the 1920's, gave up their clubhouse.[5]

The Ramgavars or A. D. L.'s leased their first clubhouse in 1917. The location was on Woodward Avenue across from what is now the Fox Theater. In 1920 the Ramgavars moved to another location as they leased a hall on Woodward Avenue in Highland Park. In 1936 the A. D. L.'s purchased a building on Hamilton in Highland Park for their new location. This clubhouse was sold in 1941.[6]

The clubhouses were gathering places for the Armenians as they not only served political purposes, but also became social centers. They were and still are places where one could meet people, talk, and play cards and backgammon. Thus many, who wouldn't set foot in a coffee house, could still have the same activities in a political clubhouse. To the Armenians of Detroit prior to World War I and even after, the clubhouses and coffee houses were among the few social outlets available.

Since the Armenians did not build their own church until 1931, the clubhouses, until this date, were the scenes of wedding ceremonies and even wedding receptions. In the early days, even into the 1920's, the level of prosperity of the Armenians allowed only sandwiches to be served at the wedding receptions.[7]

Other regular social functions of the early years extending even into the 1930's included outdoor picnics sponsored by various organizations for fund raising purposes at Palmer Park and other public parks. These picnics had to move to other locations when the holders of concessions objected to the selling of food and drinks. *Khunchooks*—food sold buffet style—were also sponsored by various organizations to raise money. At *khunchooks*, which are still given, all types of Armenian food from sheish-kebab (skewered lamb) to paklava (a rich dessert made of thin sheets of dough with nuts and other filling between the many sheets, covered by a syrup made of heavily sugared water) are sold.

In an attempt to improve their social life, some young Armenian immigrants organized an Armenian Young Men's Club in 1919. The idea was popular and soon they had rented quarters on Vernor. Membership kept growing, and the club moved to a large house on West Ferry. Some of the members boarded in the upstairs rooms and this helped to pay the rent. The club took no part in politics and men from all political parties, as well as neutrals, joined for companionship. It became a place to talk, play cards (no gambling) and other games. The club once tried to hold a dance, which failed miserably because of the absence of women. The explanation for this is that there were few single young women available at the time. The club was disbanded after fourteen years because of disinterest and because of the rise of political tempers over the Armenian Apostolic Church.[8]

There were few other Armenian sponsored dances attempted before the 1930's. All of them failed because of the absence of women.

At one of these, out of sheer boredom, some of the men started danc-ing with each other.[9] Another reason for the lack of women at the dances probably was the way relations between sexes were handled. At that time, as yet un-Americanized, social custom was to arrange a marriage with a girl's parents, the girl having little or no say about her future husband. Therefore, there was no need for a girl to go to a dance.

It was not until the middle of late 1930's when the first generation Americans came of age that dances were held successfully. With the exception of the war years, dances with Armenian and American dancing have been given successfully. The number of Armenian spon-sored dances was exceptionally large in the years after the war, as the St. John Armenian Church (see Chapter 8) erected the Armenian Cul-tural Hall on Oakman Boulevard next to the church for social and cultural activities. This, together with the Armenian Community Cen-ter, provided facilities for giving dances and the various Armenian young people's organizations that were newly organized and reorgan-ized, sponsored the dances. These organizations included the various Armenian Youth Federation chapters (young A.R.F.'s), the Armenian Church Youth Organization, the Armenian Veterans, and the A. D. L. Jrs.

5

Relief and Charity

THE ARMENIANS IN AMERICA, AS WELL AS MANY AMERI-
cans, contributed funds to help needy Armenians. In Detroit
the first organized solicitations of funds to help the needy Armenians abroad were carried out in the Detroit Armenian community
by the various Armenian political parties. Money was collected at
picnics, *khunchooks,* and at membership meetings. The Armenians of
Detroit always gave generously to these appeals to help those left behind. In 1915, for example, the Hunchaks raised five hundred dollars
to help the victims of war. Some men gave all of their meager savings
to help their fellow countrymen.[1]

The Detroit Chapter of the Armenian General Benevolent Union
was founded during World War I.[2] The Armenian General Benevolent Union was founded in Cairo, Egypt, on April 15, 1906 by
Boghos Nubar and nine other Armenians.[3] The first major act of this

charitable organization was to rush aid to homeless and stricken Armenians after Cilicia Massacre of 30,000 Armenians that was organized by the Young Turks in 1909. The A.G.B.U. also aided displaced and needy Armenians during and after World War I.[4]

Besides such emergency relief activities, the A.G.B.U. through the years has built and operated hospitals, orphanages, and schools throughout the Near East and Europe.[5] It also helped pay the cost of sending 10,000 Armenian refugees for resettlement in Soviet Armenia in the early 1930's. To help in their resettlement, the A.G.B.U. gave $500,000 to help build a model town in Armenia. Besides helping the Armenian students attending various universities in Europe,[6] the A.G.B.U. also extends subsides to ". . . scores of small denominational Armenian Apostolic, Armenian Protestant, and Armenian Catholic schools in Greece, Lebanon, and Syria."[7]

Today the international A.G.B.U. gets most of its financial support from its chapters in the United States. At present there are 117 A.G.B.U. chapters in the United States.[8] Over the years, especially since 1940, the Detroit chapter of A.G.B.U. has become the largest contributor to the international organization. The president of the international A.G.B.U. since 1953 has been Mr. Alex Manoogian of Detroit.[9] Though most of the work of the A.G.B.U. is still done abroad, the various United States chapters do some work right at home.

The Detroit chapter of the A.G.B.U. has spent $2,000 in the last two years helping needy Armenian families and university students in the Detroit area who are short of funds. The A.G.B.U. also pays twenty-five per cent of the cost of supporting the instruction of Armenian at Wayne State University.[10]

In 1910 the Dashnags organized the Armenian Relief Society (or the Armenian Red Cross). This organization also has the aim of helping needy Armenians the world over.[11] The Armenian Relief Society's Detroit Chapter also does some work in Detroit helping needy Armenian families and it also helps pay the cost of subsidizing the instruction of Armenian at Wayne State University.[12]

The Armenians who came to Detroit wanted very much to help needy Armenians in the homeland. This desire to help less fortunate Armenians was not satisfied by the work of the political parties or the A.G.B.U. in its early years. This desire to help was nationwide among the Armenians in the United States. To carry out their desires, the Armenians in the United States formed a variety of organizations to work for specific and general objects in relief, charity, and education.

The earliest of these organizations was the Sevas Auxiliary Union for Orphans, Poor Hospitals, and Culture. The Detroit chapter, organized in 1912, was the first to be formed in what became a nationwide organization. In the 1920's continuing into the 1930's, there was a great burst of activity in relief work as many organizations were formed to carry out relief and charity programs. Altogether fifteen organizations were formed. Most of these were associations of men from a certain region or town who wished to give money to help their fellow Armenians in Soviet Armenia in memory of their own town or region.

Three of these organizations, the Pan Sepastia Rehabilitation Union, the Arabkir Union, and the Malatia Educational Society, contributed money toward the establishment of towns in Soviet Armenia which bear the names Sepastia, Arabkir, and Malatia because of the funds being supplied by these organizations. Another important organization is the Armenian National Hospital Society, which supports the Savior Hospital in Constantinople. These organizations are still in existence today and some of them issue a periodical either from Philadelphia or New York.[13]

In the late 1940's the Armenian Home for the Aged was founded. The entire Armenian community contributes support to this institution, which is located on West Seven Mile Road.

6

Education

THOUGH MANY OF THE YOUNG ARMENIAN MEN WHO comprised most of Detroit's Armenian population in the period before World War I knew how to read and write some Armenian, almost all of them were totally ignorant of the English language except for a few words they had to know to get a job. Some of the Armenians who had knowledge of English tried to help their fellow Armenians by setting up a school.

The five men responsible for this school, Mr. Kanzanagian, Mr. Nishan, Mr. Ansoor, Mr. Jamison, and Mr. Arosian,[1] obtained the use of some rooms at the downtown Y. M. C. A. and classes were started in 1912. The five men named above were also the faculty of the school. Classes were given two nights a week and on Saturday and Sunday afternoon so as to give all an opportunity to attend.

Classes were offered in English, arithmetic, and Armenian citizenship. There usually were about thirty-five students attending class; however, the turnover was very high as many of the students dropped out after learning to sign their name. The school survived for eighteen months.[2]

Unfortunately not much else was done to help the people overcome the language barrier, although over the years men with the poorest command of English have learned enough to "get by." Many of the men, who knew how to read and write Armenian, taught themselves to read English.[3] However, the story is very different when it comes to foreign-born Armenian women. Detroit's female Armenian population increased tremendously in the years after World War I as the men had saved enough money to bring to the United States their wives and families and/or women to marry. As these adult women came to Detroit, they quickly slipped into the role of housekeeper. Quite a number of these women never learned the English language as they associated only with other Armenians.

Over the years, however, the problem of education in the Armenian community of Detroit has undergone a complete reversal. Today the concern is to teach the young people to read, write and speak Armenian. Various educational groups have established schools for the teaching of Armenian to the young people. The St. John Armenian Apostolic Church started an Armenian school with the completion of the Armenian Cultural Hall next door to it. The Armenian school was started in 1947. Despite these efforts, many young Armenian-Americans are growing up without even a speaking knowledge of Armenian.

In 1954 several Detroit Armenian organizations, spearheaded by the Detroit Armenian Cultural Society, started subsidizing courses in the Armenian language, which are taught at Wayne State University. Though attendance is small in these classes, all contributing groups recently decided, at a meeting of the Cultural Society, to continue to subsidize the courses.[4]

The Armenians in America, on the national level, have organized the National Association for Armenian Studies and Research. This organization is trying to raise $300,000 to endow a chair of Armenian studies at Harvard University. Many Detroiters are members of this association and in 1957 there was a dinner held in the Armenian Cultural Hall, with Professor William L. Langer as one of the speakers, in an attempt to raise funds.

7

Culture

BECAUSE OF THE LANGUAGE BARRIER, MANY DETROIT AREA Armenian immigrants were severely limited in their quest for cultural activities in the early years of the century. To meet this need, an Armenian theater developed in Detroit.

The first play presented in Detroit for an Armenian speaking audience was performed in 1914 at the Knights of Columbus Hall on Woodward Avenue. The play *Vartananz* (a play about St. Vartan and the Battle of Avaryr) was sponsored by the Detroit Chapter of the Armenian General Benevolent Union.[1]

However, a fairly regular program of Armenian plays was not started until the end of World War I. In 1918 some members of the A. R. F. organized the Ararat Democratic Society which, in 1930, became the Shant Dramatic Society.[2] Members of the Detroit Chapter of the A. D. L. Club organized a player group in 1920.[3] The two dramatic groups sponsored by the two political parties were very active in the 1920's and 1930's. They usually presented two plays each, every year. The plays presented were usually tragedies or heroic. Some of the plays presented were *The Fallen Queen, Arshag the Second, The Extinguished Lamps, The Swan Song, The Evil Soul, The Valley of Tears, For Honor, The Destroyed,* and *Daniel the Fool*.[4] The player groups also presented occasional operettas such as *Oosh Lini, Anoush Lini,* and *Arshin Mal Alan*.[5] Other organizations, such as the various charitable societies and the St. John Armenian Church Komitas Choir, sponsored plays, usually comedies, played by their own members, for fund raising purposes.[6]

Starting in the 1920's, professional Armenian actors made Detroit a regular stop on their tours of the United States. These professionals, namely Hovannes Apelian, Hovannes Zarifian, Antranig and Setrag Surabian, were all Russian Armenians. They were from Tiflis which had a large Armenian population and where the Armenian theater and arts bloomed. Coming to the United States after World War I, they made their living by touring the large centers of Armenian population in this country. The professionals did not have their own companies. Instead they recruited the actors to fill the roles in their presentations from the best of the amateur actors available in whatever city they happened to be.

It was a leisurely tour, as they would come to Detroit and stay a month or two, recruiting from the cream of the amateurs, rehearsing, and presenting their offering. The amateurs would always give their services free as the income from the one performance was all that the professionals had to show for one or two months work.[7] Hovannes Apelian, Hovannes Zarifian, and Antranig usually presented Shakespeare's works. They also performed other well-known plays, which had been translated into Armenian. The most popular were *Hamlet, Macbeth, Othello,* and Schiller's *The Robbers*.[8] Setrag Surabian was noted for comedies and operettas. Today all these men are dead and so is the professional Armenian stage.

The Highland Park High School auditorium, the Art Institute auditorium, the old Macabees Building auditorium, and the Dashnag clubhouse at 77 Victor Avenue were among the places used in presenting the plays, amateur and professional. Prices were usually a dollar for amateur performances although on occasion the admission price was fifty cents.[9] Because the one play was their only source of income for a month or two, the professionals would charge an admission of $1.50 or $2.00. Whether an amateur or professional play was given, a full house was always assured at the usual Sunday afternoon performance of a play.[10] The only advertising, besides word of mouth, were mailed circulars and advertisements in the daily Armenian language papers published in Boston and New York.[11]

The A. D. L. player group was disbanded in the late 1930's because the actors felt that they were getting too old to go on.[12] Although the Shant Dramatic Society is still in existence and still is presenting plays at the Dashnag's Armenian Community Center, it is a completely different group of players.[13] The only other organization which stills presents a play is the Knights of Vartan. Every year, on the anniversary of the Battle of Avarayr, a play, *Vantananz*, is given by them at the Armenian Cultural Hall on Oakman next to St. John Armenian Church.

In the 1920's and into the 1930's, Shah Mooradian, an internationally famous tenor in Armenian circles, gave several concerts in Detroit.[14]

After coming to Detroit in 1927, Mr. Harry Ekizian organized and directed, for the Armenian Church, the Komitas Choir. Mr. Ekizian had sung with Komitas Vartabed, the famous Armenian clergyman, composer, and arranger before Komitas became mentally unbalanced as a result of the horrors experienced at a Turkish concentration camp during World War I. Besides singing as the church choir, the Komitas Choir also gave concerts. The first of these concerts was given at Central Methodist Church in January 1928.[15] The Komitas Choir has continued to give public concerts under the direction of Mr. Harry Ekizian ever since that day.

The largest event in the musical field in the history of the Armenian community occurred on the last Sunday of 1957 as the Detroit Armenian Cultural Association co-sponsored, with the Detroit Symphony, an all Armenian program. Many organizations helped to sell tickets and assured the financial success of the concert. Alan Hovaness conducted the orchestra in the first Detroit performance of one of his recent works at this concert.

8

Religion and Politics

An overwhelming percentage of Detroit area Armenians remain loyal, in one way or another, to the Armenian Apostolic Church. Though there are many who do not attend services, let alone hold membership in one of the two churches, they were baptized in the church as infants, probably married in the church, or by a priest of the church, and, if they ever desire to go to a church service, they will go to the Armenian Apostolic Church. However, before discussing the Armenian Apostolic Church as it concerns Detroit Armenians, it must be noted that there are a number of Armenians who belong to other churches. The largest number of these Armenians are either Protestant or Catholic.

The Roman Catholic Church started proselytizing among Armenians as early as the fourteenth century when Dominican Fathers penetrated to the heart of Armenia. The Jesuits also carried on missionary work among the Armenian population of the Ottoman Empire in the seventeenth century. Another event, which cannot be overlooked as an important factor on the introduction of Catholicism to the Armenians in Cilicia, was the coming of the Crusades.[1]

Although there have been comparatively few Armenian Catholics, they have made great contributions to the preservation of Armenian culture through the work of Mekhitar and his followers. In 1717 Mekhitar founded a monastery for Armenian Catholic monks on the Island of St. Lazarus near Venice. Over the years, the monastery has amassed a large and valuable collection of books, manuscripts and works of art, as well as printing and publishing many books on Armenian history and culture. In addition, Mekhitarist monks have set up famous schools for Armenian boys in Italy, France, and Turkey.[2]

There are only a small number of Roman Catholic Armenians in the United States. In addition to Detroit, there are only five Armenian Catholic parishes organized in the United States. These parishes are in Boston; New York; Philadelphia; Patterson, New Jersey; and Los Angeles. The Boston parish, which includes about 250 families, is the largest in this country.[3]

The Detroit parish, consisting of about forty families, was organized in 1948 by The Rev. Kalajian at the invitation of Cardinal Mooney. The Rev. Kalajian is directly under Cardinal Mooney. Previous to the establishment of the parish in Detroit, Father Kogy, now Bishop Kogy of Boston, would visit Detroit periodically to hold Mass.[4] On June 3, 1958 a new $40,000 Armenian Catholic Church, located on Greenfield near Joy Road, was dedicated.

The new church building and adjoining rectory were built through the beneficence of Cardinal Mooney and the Detroit Diocese of the Catholic Church.[5] Prior to the erection of the new St. Vartan Church, the parish Masses were held in a basement chapel of Holy Redeemer Church at Vernor and Junction. The parish also had a rectory at 371 West Grand Boulevard. The rectory had a small chapel on the first floor, which was used by Father Kalajian to hold private Masses for members of the parish on weekday evenings.[6]

Today all eastern rite Roman Catholic Churches are under the leadership of Cardinal Agagianian, an Armenian. Father Kalajian was educated at the Mekhitarian College in Constantinople, studied theology and philosophy at the Catholic University in Rome. All Armenian Rite Catholic priests are ordained by Armenian Bishops.[7] Aside from the recognition of the supremacy of the Pope, there are other doctrinal differences between the Armenian Apostolic Church and the Armenian Catholic Church. However, the services of the two churches are similar. The Roman Catholic Armenian Rite services are conducted in the classical Armenian language, as are the services of the Armenian Apostolic Church. Even the music used in the services, that of Komitas and Ykmalian, is the same.[8]

The Armenian Catholics of Detroit hardly differ from the other Armenians in the Detroit area. All but one of the families is originally Turkish Armenian, and also, like the other Armenians, most are workers, but there are a few businessmen and professional people.[9]

> The first Protestant missionary societies to enter the Turkish Empire were the Church Missionary Society of England and the American Board of Commissioners for Foreign Missions. The former in 1815 sent a mission to Egypt, the latter in 1818 assigned two men to Palestine.

These first American missionaries discovered that of all the peoples of the Ottoman Empire, the Armenians ". . . were the most open to Protestant missionary influences."[10] In the 1840's the Armenian Apostolic Church became alarmed at the growing number of Armenians being converted by the missionaries. The church acted by starting to excommunicate those who remain loyal to the Protestants. Also, the church, with its civil power over the Armenian population under the millet system of the Ottoman Empire, encouraged persecution of those people remaining loyal to the Protestants. The persecution was very effective, as Protestant Armenians were socially ostracized and were deprived of their rights to engage in commerce.[11]

Though the persecution was halted with the intervention of the Turkish government when the Armenian Catholicos Matthew declared: "Religion is free in Turkey," on May 17, 1846; on June 21, 1846 Matthew issued a bill of perpetual excommunication and anathema against all Protestant Armenians. As a result of this, on June 25, 1846, a conference was convoked which drew up a constitution for the Armenian Evangelical Church, which was halfway between Congregationalism and Presbyterianism.[12] The reason for this type of constitution was to give the missionaries some measure of control as they felt that the people were not yet quite ready to guide themselves.[13]

These are twenty-seven Protestant Armenian Churches in the United States at the present time. They are associated in the Armenian Evangelical Union of America. The organization is divided into two sections, eastern and western. The Detroit Armenian Congregational Church belongs to the eastern states section consisting of thirteen churches.[14] In 1946 the total number of Protestants of Armenian descent in the United States was ". . . roughly estimated at 10,000."[15]

An Armenian Congregational Church was organized by a group of young Armenian immigrants in 1912. They obtained the use of a chapel in the Central Methodist Church at Woodward and Adams for services. Mr. Kanzanagian, Dr. G. Attarian, Mr. Jamison (Catholic at the time) and Mr. Kaian took turns preaching. The church organization died for lack of interest in eighteen months.[16] There was, however, other Evangelical work performed by volunteer Armenian pastors and teachers who then lived in the city.[17] "Organized Evangelical work started in Detroit in 1919. . . ." This has evolved into what is today the Detroit Armenian Congregational Church. Before they were able to purchase their own church building, the Congregational Church at various times used the facilities at Woodward and Davison,[18] and a basement chapel in the Highland Park Congregational Church.[19] Meanwhile another group of ". . . Armenian Protestants were meeting separately at the Trinity Methodist Church in Highland Park under the leadership of the Rev. Abraham Shirinian." During the pastorate of the The Rev. Y. K. Rushdouni (1923–1930) the two groups united as the Armenian Congregational Church.[20]

In 1927, with the assistance of an interdenominational citizens committee, chaired by Tracey W. McGregor and including such prominent citizens as Judge Alexis C. Angell, Fred M. Butzel, and Rabbi Leo M. Franklin, among others,[21] the Armenian Congregational Church purchased a church building at Hamilton and Collingwood for $18,500.[22] In 1952 the Congregational Church, feeling the need for more room, purchased a church building and parish house at Davison and Twelfth Street from the Twelfth Street Evangelical Brethren Church for $80,000. The new church was dedicated on October 19, 1952.[23]

The Rev. Tovmassian, minister of the Armenian Congregational Church, estimates that there are approximately one hundred and fifty families of Armenian descent holding to the Congregational Church. About one hundred of the families take an active part in church activities. Since the Congregational Church has a smaller base of support than either of the two Armenian Apostolic Churches, the members of the church must pay a greater portion of their income to support the church.[24]

The Congregational Church services are conducted in Armenian, although the sermon may be in English at times for the benefit of those who cannot understand Armenian. Although the services are conducted in Armenian, they have no connection with the services of the Armenian Apostolic Church as they are only a translation of a Congregational service.

The reason for the brevity of the discussion on the Detroit Armenian Catholic Church and the Detroit Armenian Congregational Church is that, except for certain individuals among the Armenian Catholics and Protestants, these groups have had little, if any, effect on the development of the rest of the Armenian community.[25]

The first Armenian Apostolic Church service in the United States was held on July 12, 1889 in Worcester, Massachusetts. Less than two years later, on January 18, 1891, the Worcester Armenian community consecrated the first Armenian Church in America. On October 16, 1898 ". . . an encyclical of the Catholicos of all Armenians, Mukurtich Khrimian Hairik was solemnly read in the Armenian Church at Worcester, and the American Diocese of the Armenian Church was established." An encyclical in 1928 established California as a separate Diocese.[26]

The first Armenian Apostolic Church service conducted in Detroit was held in a church at Erie and Anderson in Delray, in 1908. The service was conducted by an Armenian priest who stopped off for a few days in Detroit while travelling to his destination.[27] However, it was not until 1913 that the Armenian community of Detroit organized a parish ands petitioned the North American Diocese of the Armenian Church to send a priest. Due to lack of funds, Mr. Peter Manoogian paid, out of his pocket, the $275 fare for The Rev. Sahag Nazeretian to come to Detroit to be its first Armenian priest.

The community, having no church building, secured, again through the efforts of Mr. Manoogian, the use of St. John Episcopal Church[28] at Woodward and High Street (now Vernor Highway) for service on Sunday afternoons.[29] The ten years of The Rev. Nazaretian's pastorate were not prosperous ones for the Detroit Parish of the Armenian Church. Attendance at the church services in St. John Episcopal Church was usually very small. Tray collections reflected the poor attendance as the tray collections on some Sundays would total less than a dollar in the years before World War I. Another reason for the low collections was the poor economic status of the people at that time. At Christmas and Easter many more people would attend and the tray collections would total about two hundred dollars. The Rev. Nazaretian's salary was supposed to be twenty-five dollars a week but he was rarely paid on time.[30] However, as World War I came and passed, and as the 1920's went by, the finances of the Armenian population improved and the financial condition of the parish reflected this improvement.

Late in the 1920's the congregation voted on a proposal, favored by the priest, to buy a church building near Third and Fort Streets for forty of forty-five thousand dollars. The congregation voted against the proposal.[31] There were other proposals made to buy a church building, but these never came to a vote.[32]

From 1923 to 1932, except for the year 1929, the Detroit Armenian parish had two priests. Detroit obtained its second priest and its new pastor in an unusual manner, as The Rev. Hachik Kroozian became the first Armenian priest to be ordained in Detroit in April of 1923.[33] Detroit needed at least two priests in the 1920's and 1930's and needs even more today as it has the largest Armenian population between the two coasts. There were, and still are, many small communities of Armenians in various mid-western cities that have asked, or still ask, Detroit's assistance in holding Armenian Church services. In the 1920's and 1930's Grand Rapids, Cleveland,[34] and Pontiac[35] appealed to Detroit for such help. The Detroit Parish regularly sent a priest to that city.[36] Today this practice of loaning out a priest is still continued as the Detroit Parish Council sends a priest to Cleveland once a month.[37]

The autumn of 1930 saw two temporary changes occur in regard to the church. The Rev. Atig Dzotsikian reported to the Parish Council that, due to the distance and the odd hours of the services at St. John Episcopal Church, he thought it would be more advantageous, in terms of community attendance, to move the services to the Ferris School on Cortland in Highland Park.[38] The school auditorium was consecrated and church services were held at the school every Sunday for one year starting November 7, 1930.[39]

The other change decided upon by the Parish Council was the organization of another church to service the Delray community of Armenians. This was originally recommended by The Rev. Dzotsikian at the same time that he recommended using the Ferris School.[40] To implement this move, it was decided that a Delray Parish Council should be elected.[41] The Delray Parish Council was to conduct its business separately, though there were to be joint meetings of the two councils to coordinate their activities.[42] In March of 1931, the Delray Parish Council obtained the use of the Hungarian Church in Delray for Sunday services.[43] The Detroit Parish Council decided the priest should hold Mass in Delray at least every other week.[44]

However, the plans proved unsuccessful as on April 30, 1931, less than two months after all had been arranged, the Detroit Parish Council decided that Delray was a part of the Detroit community and that the Detroit Parish Council would carry on the work in that area. The Delray Parish Council was dissolved.[45] The services that were held in Delray at this time, and for the additional short period of time until the split in the community, were held in the Armenian Revolutionary Federation's Zavarian Hall in Delray.[46]

The Armenians of Detroit very much wanted their own church building. In the late 1920's a first step was taken in this direction with the purchase of a lot on Hamilton near Glendale. However, the Parish Council was unable to overcome the objections of neighbors to the building of the church and were forced to sell the lot. The church lost $2,000 when it sold the property.[47] On March 28, 1930 the building committee reported to the rest of the Parish Council that they had purchased the deed to a lot on Oakman Boulevard between LaSalle and Fourteenth Street. The committee went on to recommend the construction of a $25,000 church building that summer, reporting that $10,000 to $12,000 could be borrowed and that the rest could be raised by the Parish Council with the help of the $2,500 in the treasury of the Ladies Auxiliary.[48] Four months later the building committee reported to the Parish Council that, with the prevailing unemployment, there should be no construction undertaken.[49]

The desire to build a church was still strong and The Rev. Atig Dzotsikian, who became the new pastor of the church in August of 1930, in less than four months visited 271 homes, blessing them, correcting addresses, and carrying on a campaign for the building of a church.[50] By December 5th of the same year, The Rev. Dzotsikian, continuing his energetic pace, had visited 430 homes.[51] The Rev. Dzotsikian was not the only person engaged in a door to door campaign. From 1929 to 1931 a fund raising committee of the church went on a house to house campaign raising money and they obtained pledges and cash ranging from three dollars to seven hundred dollars.[52] In this effort to raise funds, the church also sponsored picnics[53] and concerts by the Komitas Church Choir at Highland Park School.[54]

Despite the depression, it was decided to go ahead with the building of the church in the summer of 1931. Accordingly, on Sunday, August 2, 1931, a ceremony was held by the congregation at the site of the church as the four cornerstones of the building were blessed.[55] The building, costing $31,000[56] was finished that autumn and on

November 22, 1931, with Archbishop Leon Tourian officiating, the church was consecrated St. John the Baptist Armenian Apostolic Church. A dedication banquet was held that night at Webster Hall with the Archbishop as guest of honor.[57]

While the church was being built, and even after its completion, the congregation was suffering financial troubles. On July 15, 1931, for example, the treasury of the church was temporarily bankrupt.[58] On August 5th of the same year, the Parish Council found that there was not enough money in the treasury to pay the priest.[59] On January 28, 1932, not only the plight of the church, but the welfare and the economic plight of the Armenians in the community, was discussed at the Parish Council meeting.[60] The financial situation of church hit bottom in 1932 as the total receipts for the year fell $260 short of total expenditures.[61] The deacon and the pastor both took voluntary pay cuts to help the church.[62]

The contractor for the building of the church had starting construction only after five members of the church, Mr. Peter Manoogian, Dr. Garabed Attarian, Mr. Charles Sultanian, Dr. Dermanjian, and The Rev. Dzotsikian had personally underwritten the church's note. In 1933, the church fell behind on its payments and the contractor seized the bank accounts of the five men. However, with the help of the congregation, the Parish Council managed to raise enough money to pay the contractor and allow the men to retain their money.[63]

On August 17, 1933, The Rev. Atig Dzotsikian tendered his resignation to the Parish Council.[64] Action on the resignation was delayed, but on September 28, 1933, the Parish Council of St. John Armenian Church accepted the resignation.[65] From subsequent events this appears to foreshadow what was to happen on December 24, 1933. Sunday of that date saw the assassination of Archbishop Leon Tourian while he was conducting services at the Holy Cross Armenian Church on New York City.[66] The nine men arrested and later convicted of this crime were members of the Armenian Revolutionary Federation (Dashnaktzoutzyoune).[67] Two of them, Matios Lelegian and Nishan Sarkissian, were sentenced to death while the other seven were given twenty-year sentences.[68] Governor Herbert Lehman later commuted the two death sentences to life imprisonment.[69]

This murder of Archbishop Tourian signaled a deep schism among the Armenian people in the United States and in other Armenian communities of the world outside of Soviet Armenia. Detroit was not spared and this schism exists even today. The events leading up to this split in the Armenian communities of the world are complex and require a monograph to do them justice. However, for the purpose of this paper, it is hoped that the following sketch will suffice.

A good place to begin the sketch is the revolutionary ferment to secure an independent Armenia. The revolutionary ferment was carried on by the various political parties which were formed in the nineteenth and twentieth centuries. All of these political parties, despite their seeming differences, had the same basic aim: the independence of Turkish Armenia. This drive for independence by the Armenians came as a result of the Armenian "awakening" of knowledge and ideas in the middle of the nineteenth century. This "awakening" was the result of the efforts of the Armenians, not only in Turkey, but in Russia, Italy, France, India, or wherever there was an Armenian colony.

The first revolutionary organization was founded in 1880 after the Bayazid and Alaskered massacres. It was called the "Defenders of the Fatherland." This organization was short-lived as two years later the government discovered its existence and imprisoned seventy-five persons. [70] The Armenagans were a fully developed organization by 1885 in the district of Van. Besides educational activities, the Armenagans were a trained fighting group that fought and defended the city of Van during the massacres of the late 1890's.[71] This is not the end of the Armenagans, but to better relate its history, it is necessary to go to the story of the Hunchaks. A group of Armenian students in Geneva started putting out a newspaper *Hunchak* (The Bell) in November 1887. The name of the party was thus derived.[72] Nazarbek, the leader of this group and his few followers

> . . . hoped to start a great insurrectionary movement in Turkey. Nazarbek envisaged drawing the Assyrians, Yizidis and even the Kurds (!) into the movement and planned to cooperate with the Macedonian, Cretan and Albanian revolutionaries. Then, ultimately, it might be possible to unite Turkish, Russian and Persian Armenians in one socialist state.[73]

By 1890 the party had revolutionary cells in various parts of the Ottoman Empire.[74] The party had also spread to the United States by 1890 as supporting branches were organized in Boston and Worcester.[75]

The Hunchaks split in 1896 as one faction of the party, the Veragazmial or Reformed Hunchaks, disavowed the socialist plank in the party platform.[76] The Veragazmials, the Armenagans, and Armenian patriotic unions in the Balkans and other countries united to form the Ramgavar Party.[77] In October of 1921, the Ramgavars united with the Veragazmial Hunchaks who had become the Azadagans or Liberals and formed the Armenian Democratic Liberal Party.[78] The Ramgavars abandoned killing, except in war.[79] The Hunchak Party with its socialist platform, but minus the terrorism, still exists today, though it is very weak.

The strongest, most active Armenian political party in the United States, and perhaps in some areas outside the United States, is the Armenian Revolutionary Federation. The A. R. F. was born in Russia in a period when the Armenians were being suppressed by Czar Alexander III and Pobiedonostsev.

> Their [Armenian] schools were closed, their newspapers censored and their Church persecuted. The effect of this was to drive the national and revolutionary movement under-ground. Student groups in St. Petersburg and Moscow came under the influence of the Russian socialists and terrorists. In Tiflis they organized secret groups, which read Darwin, Spencer, Lassalle and Marx. In the summer of 1890 these groups, after many heated discussions and clashes, combined to from the Armenian Revolutionary Federation or Dashnagtzuotian. . . . The essential plank in the platform was action to secure the "political and economic freedom of Turkish Armenia."[80]

To bring this about, the A. R. F. ". . . arranged to organize revolutionary band which should fight the government incessantly and should terrorize government officials, traitors, userers, and all kinds of exploiters."[81] The Dashnags did not become active until 1895, and as the Hunchaks split about this time, the Dashnags soon became the dominant and best organized Armenian political party.[82]

The Dashnags continued to be the leading revolutionary group as the twentieth century came, and brought World War I, which saw the Turkish government institute, and carry out, a policy of extermination against the Armenians.[83] In 1918 Russian Armenia was declared an independent republic.[84] The government was dominated by Dashnags, but all Armenians, regardless of political affiliation, united to support the newly founded Republic. However, the weak and small Republic was unable to fight off the continual advances of a reviving

Turkey under the leadership of Ataturk. By 1920 it was apparent that Armenia was crumbling and would soon fall to Turkey. Fortunately for the Armenians in Armenia, for any alternative is better than Turkish rule, the Soviets moved in on December 2, 1920, [85] and Armenia became one of the Soviet Republics.[86]

With the Soviets coming in, there was nothing left for the Dashnags to do but leave Armenia. Thus the Dashnag party suddenly found itself out of power, though outside of Soviet Armenia, it now tried to gain control over the Armenians in the "diaspora" with the use of the one institution that held all Armenians together, the Armenian Apostolic Church.[87]

Attacking clergymen and the church was nothing new to the Dashnags. They had been fighting the church since 1896 because they felt it was necessary to break the power of the church in order to secure control over the mass of Armenians.[88]

Attacks began against Archbishop Tourian even before he reached the United States after his election as the Primate of the Church. There was "nothing personal" in these attacks as Archbishop Tourian was attacked by the Dashnags only because he stood for the church and its continued independence from politics.[89] The verbal and printed attacks on Archbishop Tourian mounted until they led to outright physical attack.

After the Archbishop's assassination, the Dashnags left the North American Diocese of the Armenian Church, succeeding in taking a few churches, where their members gave them control over the Church Parish Council, with them. The Dashnags then proceeded to set up their own organization known as the Armenian National Apostolic Church of America. Today there are fourteen churches affiliated with this organization.[90]

In the years immediately following the end on World War II, there was a serious attempt made by both sides to heal the schism in the

Armenian communities of the United States. This attempt was made possible by conditions that existed at that time. The Dashnags had based (and still do) much of their anti-church campaigns on charges that, as long as the Catholicos resides in Soviet Armenia, the church would be under Russian communistic domination. Friendly relations between the United States and Russia, during and immediately after World War II, lessened the effect of this accusation. Because of the actions of some of its leaders, the A. R. F. came to be associated in the minds of many people with the fascist movement just when anti-fascist feeling was running high.[91] Finally, because of its low level of popularity among Armenians, and because the organization seemed to have no further or present basis for existence, many members of the A. R. F. were dropping out of the organization.[92]

On the other side, the church has always been anxious to somehow heal the schism in the community. In 1947 the Catholicos sent to Archbishop Tiran Nersoyan of the North American Diocese of the Armenian Apostolic Church a letter vesting the Archbishop all necessary authority to reunify the Armenian community. The North American Diocese of the Church held an assembly to decide if there should be an attempt at reunion. Though the A. D. L.'s in the assembly vigorously opposed such a move, the Diocese decided to continue negotiations aimed at reunification.

On their part, the Dashnag Churches dissolved their national church organization and elected a three-man committee, which had the necessary authority to reunify the Dashnag Churches with the North American Diocese. Negotiations were well under way when the Truman Doctrine was declared and all semblance of friendship between the United States and the Soviet Union were ended. The Dashnags broke off the negotiations as the international situation made the outlook brighter for their efforts to seize control of the church.[93] The situation has deteriorated rapidly since that period as the schism has grown wider and feelings have grown more bitter on both sides.[94]

The struggle is not just between the Dashnags and the church. A staunch supporter of the church throughout the world is the Armenian Democratic Liberal Party. While the Dashnags are stronger than the A. D. L. party in the United States, the opposite is true in other parts of the world, especially in Armenian communities in some of the countries in the Near East.[95] The Dashnag charge that all anti-Dashnags are pro-Communist is the main propaganda line. This malicious charge is taken as the truth by some people who are unaware of the facts. A typical Dashnag statement is one, which follows. The writer is Reuben Darbinian, editor in chief of Hairenik, the Dashnag press of the United States, and the foremost Dashnag in the world.

> Among the communist advocates of the free world there are also those who have chosen this path, not because they naively believe that by doing so they can achieve their political or natural aims. . . . To this class also belong the leaders of the Armenian Ramgavars, the intellectuals who slink around the Armenian General Benevolent Union, who blindly believe, or want to believe that by tying their kite to Soviet twine they can "injure" Turkey, or "help" Armenia, or save the Armenian Church and especially inflict a mortal blow to the Armenian Revolutionary Federation.[96]

In this excerpt, Mr. Darbinian, as will be noticed, attacks the non-political A. G. B. U. The probable reason for the "dislike" of the A. G. B. U. is that the A. R. F. cannot control it and use it for its own end.

In 1956 the Dashnags succeeded in seizing the sub-Catholicosate of Antillas in Lebanon. The control of this important religious center gives the Dashnag churches throughout the world a "peg" of seeming legitimacy and further deepens the schism. Following the seizure of the sub-Catholicosate, the Dashnags sent, from Antilias, Archbishop Khoren Paroyian to the United States in an unsuccessful attempt to win churches away from Etchmiadzin. Following are some excerpts from an article in the *New York Times* that obviously was written from a strictly Dashnag point of view by an unknowing reporter. The article has a Boston dateline.

> Tomorrow, Archbishop Khoren Paroyian, prelate of Beirut, is to arrive here to assume authority over Armenian Apostolic churches in the United States. There are about 300,000 members of the church in this country. . . .
>
> Since 1933, the American diocese has been shorn of Catholicate leadership because Armenian Americans have insisted that Soviet political doctrine should not be filtered to the free world through Armenian Churches.
>
> A solution to the problem came last February, when non-Communist Armenian communities in the Middle East chose Zarah, Bishop of Aleppo, as Catholicos. As Bishop, he had demonstrated his determination to keep the church independent of politics and in its democratic tradition.[97]

On October 20, 1957, the *New York Times* published an article on a rebuttal issued by The Rev. Megherian of the North American Diocese of the Armenian Apostolic Church.

The Boston group [the Armenian National Apostolic Church of America—the Dashnag church organization] is not listed in the *Yearbook of American Churches*. According to the Religious news service, it is a minority group with twelve or sixteen churches, mainly in New England. Referring to the fact that the seat of his church is in Soviet Armenia, Father Megherian said:

"Political regimes have come and gone but the Supreme Spiritual See of the Armenian people since 301 A.D. has remained in or tended to return to Etchmiadzin, Armenia. Consequently, devout Armenians all over the world, while regretting the political regime now operative on Armenia, remain spiritually faithful to the Supreme Patriarch of the Church.

"It would be a grave mistake to forsake the Christian elements of Armenia; yet that is what the members of the projected schismatic diocese are trying to do.

"The mother church will resist all efforts to subordinate religion to the political dictates of any group whatever. The sole loyalty of the members of the true Armenian Church in America is the Government of the United States."[98]

In Detroit one could observe the "build up" to the schism and all the resulting effects. However, passions over the murder of Archbishop Tourian did not reach the crest that it did on other communities. Though The Rev. Dzotsikian's resignation was accepted on September 28, 1933, less than three months before the murder, there was at the time no ill feeling between the pro-Dashnag priest and the

Parish Council as evidenced by the tea party given for The Rev. Dzotsikian by the Parish Council; this came to be later.

Five days after the assassination of Archbishop Tourian, the Parish Council of St. John Armenian Church decided to hold a special requiem for the late Archbishop. The service was to be followed by a protest meeting.[99] The intensity with which the Armenian people of Detroit regarded the murder can be judged by the capacity crowds of Armenians who attended the protest meetings in the Northern, Cass Technical, and Highland Park High School auditoriums.[100]

Following the assassination, there had been conversations carried on between the Detroit Dashnag leaders and the Parish Council. The Dashnags stated that they did not want the community split over the church. If the Parish Council would accept four Dashnag members to the body, (the Parish Council was made up of nine men at this time) the Dashnags would not do anything to split the community. If the Parish Council refused the offer, the Dashnags said that they would go out and solicit church membership among members of the Dashnaktzoutyuon and seize control of the church at the general membership meeting when the election of officers came up.

The Parish Council refused the Dashnag offer and told Dashnag leaders to bring their members to the membership meeting of the church and let whichever side having the most votes win. The Dashnags never showed up at the membership meeting.[101] They never came back to the church after Archbishop Tourian's murder.[102]

There was another incident that shows the bitterness over Tourian's murder at that particular time. The former pastor, The Rev. Dzotsikian, sent the Parish Council two derogatory letters which angered the council. The Parish Council protested to The Rev. Dzotsikian and demanded that he retract all the allegations he made in the letters.[103]

On March 27, 1934, the Parish Council accepted the resignation of The Rev. Bedros Mampreian, assistant pastor under The Rev. Dzotsikian and acting pastor at the time.[104] The Rev. Mempreian became the pastor of the church set up by the Detroit Dashnags. In 1941 the Dashnags moved the location of their church services from the Zavarian Club in Delray to the newly purchased Armenian Community Center.[105] The church was given the name St. Sarkis and to the present day, it still rents the second floor of the Dashnag Center.[106]

Thus, there are two Armenian Apostolic Churches in Detroit. Both churches conduct the exact same service in the classical Armenian language. The only difference between the two churches is their allegiance.[107] St. John Armenian Church is in the Detroit Council of Churches.

The Diocese of the Armenian Apostolic Church of North America, a member of the national Council of Churches, comprises thirty-nine churches (two of these are in Canada). In addition the separate California Diocese is comprised of nine churches. This makes a total of forty-eight Armenian Apostolic churches that remain loyal to Etchmiadzin.[108] All of these parishes have their own church buildings.[109] The same cannot be said about the fourteen Dashnag churches. Some of the Dashnag churches, Detroit and Niagara Falls, for example, are located in Dashnag clubhouses. This is an indication of the relative strengths of the two opposing sides in terms of popular and financial support from the Armenian people.

In 1946 the North American Diocese established the Armenian Church Youth Organization of America. The A. C. Y. O. A. is a democratic organization which is headed by elected officers. The governing body of the national organization is the Central Council, which is composed of nine members, two of whom are Detroiters.[110] The A. C. Y. O. A. is a vigorous supporter of the church and denounces its enemies.

St. John Armenian Church is still located on Oakman Boulevard. In 1946 the Armenian Cultural Hall, a two-story structure costing $175,000, was erected on an adjoining lot. The second floor of the building is used as a church on religious holidays to handle the large attendance. Bishop Sion Manoogian, pastor of St. John Church from 1946 to 1952, supplied the leadership necessary for the erection of the Cultural Hall. Bishop Manoogian left Detroit to become Primate of the Armenian Apostolic Church of South America. Because of the growing membership and the shift in population, St. John Armenian Church will soon move to a new site on James Couzens Highway and Southfield Road. A larger church and cultural building, costing a million dollars, will be erected at this location.

The international schism in the Armenian communities outside of Soviets Armenia appears as though it will endure as long as there is a cold war. Without a cold war for Dashnags to use as a background to their charges on communism against all who oppose them, the Dashnags will rapidly lose strength, as illustrated by what happened after World War II.

It is a sad spectacle to see this split and all the name calling within as small an ethnic group as the Armenians. They are loyal American citizens who have prospered in this country. It would be more constructive if the energies spent fighting one another could be channeled into helping the needy Armenians if the Near East who have suffered greatly since World War I. The split in Detroit will heal when the international schism heals or when the process of assimilation of the Armenians is complete, whichever comes first.

From reading this paper one might conclude that all Armenians are on one side or another of this issue. This is not true. Much of the Armenian population in Detroit and the United States is either ignorant of the issue or is indifferent to it. This is especially true of younger people.

Though there was violence in New York and in other parts of the world, it did not reach Detroit. In Detroit, as elsewhere, though Armenians may quarrel over the church, they remain friends on the individual level.

The Early Detroit
Armenian Community and
St. John Armenian Apostolic Church

Fealty Pledged by Armenians

4,000 Attend Native Music Festival

A resolution in which the Armenian Democratic Liberal Party pledged itself to continue its support of American ideals and institutions and to defend the "American Constitution and Government against the onslaughts of unAmerican influences and activ.ies," was unanimously passed Sunday afternoon by officers of the organization.

The organization has been holding its fifteenth annual national convention in Detroit since July 3. An executive committee composed of naturalized citizens was formed by the convention whose purpose is to preach and disseminate the ideals of democracy among the Armenian people. Capt. James Chankalian, of New York, a Spanish War veteran and one of the troops who fought on the Caucasian and Palestine fronts during the World War, was elected a member of this committee.

More than 4,000 persons attended the music and dancing festival Sunday afternoon at the State Fair Grounds which climaxed the convention.

Mme. Rose Zullalian, of Boston, contralto, singing Armenian folk songs, featured the afternoon program. Mme. Zullalian was dressed in an Armenian costume of purple velvet embroidered with gold and valued at $4,000. Komitas, Armenian choral union of Detroit, sang native songs and presented native dances, while the high spot of the evening's entertainment was reached when an Armenian old country wedding was presented. All of the participants were dressed in native wedding costumes and the service was preached in the native tongue. Dancing to American music followed the program.

The organization has no connection with American political parties, officers pointed out. The word "Democratic" in the title refers to the democratic form of government and not to the party. Dr. Leon Mughalian, of Chicago, presided at the meetings. Nishan Nelbandian is president of the Detroit branch.

The largest gathering of Armenians for any affair in the history of Detroit's Armenian community. Estimates are 6,000 to 7,000. The occasion was the 15th Annual Convention of the Armenian Democratic Liberal Organization at the State Fairgrounds in Detroit on July 7, 1935. The event was filmed by Jack Stevens (Hagop DerStepanian), and has been converted into video. (Poster of the event on the following page)

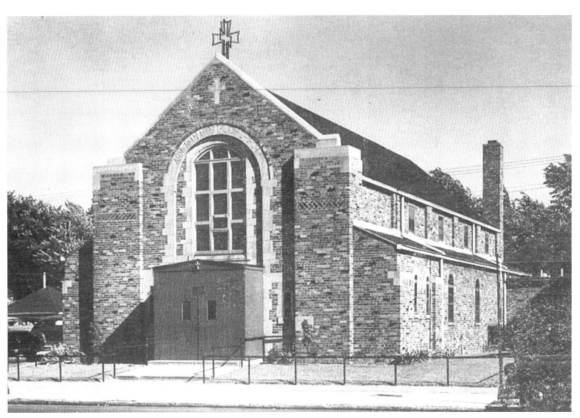

St. John Armenian Church, built 1931 on Oakman Blvd. in Detroit.

Dedication of St. John by Archbishop Tourian, the Primate of the Eastern Diocese. Rev. Fr. Atig Dzotsikian to his right. Rev. Fr. Bedros Mamprian to his left. Nov. 22, 1931.

The faithful gathered at the St. John Church entrance for the dedication. Nov. 22, 1931.

A rare photograph of early Armenians in Detroit. Picture was taken on the doorsteps of Y.M.C.A., in 1913. Many of them served in the Parish Council of St. John Armenian Church.

St. John interior.

First Cultural Building, adjacent to St. John on Oakman Blvd.

Armenian Bishop Here
For Dedication Rites

(MIRROR photo)

ARMENIAN CHURCH DEDICATED. — The new Armenian Apostolic Episcopalian church, 1335 Oakman blvd., was dedicated yesterday before 1,500 persons by (l. to r.) Rev. Atig Zatzigian, Bishop Leon Tourain of New York, and other high officials.

NEW ARMENIAN CHURCH OPENED

Hovanes Mugrvich Apostolic Congregation Dedicates Building.

About 1,500 of Detroit's Armenians crowded into and around the Hovanes Mugrvich Armenian Apostolic Church Sunday when Bishop Leon Tourian, of New York, head of the church in the Americas, officiated at the rites of dedication.

Assisting Bishop Tourian at the altar were the pastor of the local church, the Rev. Atig Dzotzigian, and his assistant, the Rev. Bedros Mampreian.

The service was sung by a choir vested in the ancient Armenian choir robes, under the direction of Harry Ekezian, choirmaster.

MASS OFFERED.

Bishop Tourian dedicated the church to Hovanes Maugrvich, or St. John the Baptist. Following the dedication of the altar and the church he offered mass.

The dedication of the church was the fulfillment of the dreams of a little group of Armenians who organized the Detroit congregation in 1914.

The services of the church were held in the chapel of St. John's Episcopal Church until last year, when the congregation moved to the Ferry School, Highland Park, pending the completion of the new building.

The new church is the first to be erected in Michigan by an Armenian Apostolic congregation.

Dr. M. K. Mihran is chairman of the building committee, which ? been working for the building ? past five years. Other officers of t committee are: Charles Martin, s? retary; Y. H. Gononian, treasur and George G. Sohigian, auditor

HEAD OF COMMITTEE.

The trustees of the congregati are A. Ajemian, chairman, and Bakerjian and Oscar Boshnakian

A banquet, celebrating the dedic tion of the church, was held at We ster Hall Sunday night.

Archbishop Ghevont Tourian (1879–1933), Primate of the Eastern Diocese, 1931–1933. Consecrated St. John Armenian Apostolic Church on Oakman Blvd. in Detroit.

Clergy of the Detroit Armenian Apostolic Church from 1924–1950

Rev. Sahag Nazaretian
1913–1922

Fr. Bedros Mampreian
1922–1932

Fr. Hachik Kroozian
1922–1924

Rt. Rev. Vahram Nazaretian
1924–1928

Fr. Atig Dzotsikian
1930–1934

Bishop Vartan Kasparian
1934–1937

Fr. Vahan Jelalian
1937–1941

Fr. Nerses Odian
1941–1947

Rev. Isahag Ghazarian
1948–1951

Very Rev. Fr. Sion Manoogian
1946–1952
(Later Archbishop,
Primate of the Eastern Diocese)

Mr. Alex Manoogian and Mr. Edward Mardigian are remembered beyond the Detroit Armenian community for their philanthropic contributions. In the Detroit Armenian community, their leadership, enthusiasm and generosity were major factors in the creation of the St. John Armenian complex.

Mr. Alex Manoogian

Mr. Edward Mardigian

Blessing of the ground for the Southfield St. John Church and new Cultural Hall on Sunday, June 19, 1960. His Holiness Catholicos Vasken I officiating.

Blessing of the ground at the Southfield location of St. John by Catholicos Vasken I, Catholicos of all Armenians, in June 1960. On left, Mr. Alex Manoogian and on right, Mr. Edward Mardigian.

Church under construction, Mr. Suren Pilafian, architect.

The Church was consecrated on Sunday, Nov. 20, 1966. His Grace Bishop Torkom Manoogian (now Patriarch of Jerusalem), to his right. Rev. Fr. Arnak Kasparian, to his left, Very Rev. Fr. Yeghishe Gizirian (now Archbishop) and Rev. Fr. Diran Papazian.

Consecration of the altar (constructed in Italy) and the altar painting (not pictured) by His Holiness on Sunday, May 12, 1968.

His Holiness Vasken I on the occasion of the altar consecration. To his right, Rev. Fr. Diran Papazian. To his left, Very Rev. Fr. Nerses Bozabalian (now Archbishop) and Very Rev. Fr. Yeghishe Gizirian (now Archbishop).

His Holiness Vasken I (1908–1994), Catholicos of all Armenians from 1955–1994, the longest reign in Armenian church history. His remarkable reign outlasted communist atheism and saw the independence and rebirth of the Republic of Armenia.

St. John Armenian Apostolic Church, Southfield, Michigan.

View of the altar.

Altar painting by Zubel Kachadoorian.

St John building complex

St John with adjoining Cultural Hall.

Entrance to the Alex and Marie Manoogian Museum and the Edward and
Helen Mardigian Library

Armenian-American Veterans' Memorial Building

A.G.B.U. Alex & Marie Manoogian School

SAINT JOHN'S ARMENIAN CHURCH AND CULTURAL CENTER

Suren Pilafian
Architect

In the years 1950 to 1956, the Executive Committee of the Apostolic Society met to discuss plans for the proposed new St. John Church and Cultural Center that was to be built on a sixteen acre site on Northwestern Highway in Southfield. This is an artist's sketch of the proposal.

1940's Armenian Home for the Aged located on West Seven Mile Road in Livonia.

Takvor and Takouhi Manoogian Manor (Michigan Home for the Armenian Aged) located on Middlebelt Road in Livonia. Named in honor of Mr. Alex Manoogian's parents.

Mr. & Mrs. Alex Manoogian gifted their home, located on the Detroit River, to the City of Detroit in 1962 to be used as the residence for the mayor. It is referred to by the media as the "Manoogian Mansion."

Gomitas Vartabed Monument. Downtown Detroit, East Jefferson Ave. near Woodward. Father Gomitas (1869–1935), foremost composer and Ethnomusicologist of the Armenian Nation. Imprisoned on April 24, 1915 by the Turkish government. Though released from prison, he never fully recovered from witnessing the genocide of his people. He died in Paris.

Day of unveiling, June 21, 1981.

Armenian Memorial Shrine, the Etchmiazdin Monument, Woodlawn Cemetery, Detroit.
Unveiled 1963.

The Urn of Tears. Woodlawn Cemetery. The concepts and projects of the Urn of Tears and the Armenian Memorial Shrine (preceding page) were spearheaded by then St. John pastor Rev. Fr. Diran Papazian.

NOTES

Chapter 1

1 Leon Arpee, *A History of Armenian Christianity* (New York: The Armenian Missionary Association of America, Inc., 1946), p. 9.

2 *Ibid.*, p. 15.

3 Vardepet Yeghisheh, *The Epic of St. Vardan the Brave*, abridged translation by C. F. Neumann, commentary by Vahan M. Kurkjian (New York: Diocese of the Armenian Church in North America, 1951), p. 9.

4 Jacques De Morgan, *History of the Armenian People*, trans. Ernest F. Barry (Boston: Hairenik [no date[), p. 135.

5 Arpee, *op. cit.*, p. 50.

6 De Morgan, *op. cit.*, p. 136.

7 Arpee, *op. cit.*, pp. 75–89.

8 A. A. Sarkissian, *History of the Armenian Question to 1885* (Urbana: The University of Illinois Press, 1938), pp. 12–14.

9 H. B. Boghosian, *Highlights in Armenian History* (Pasadena: Dr. H. B. Boghosian, 1957), p. 165.

10 *Ibid.*, pp.12–13.

11 Bureau of the Census, *Fifteenth Census of the United States 1930*, Vol. II "Population" (Washington: Government Printing Office, 1933), p. 347. The figures for 1920 and 1910 are 37,647 and 23,938 respectively.

12 Bureau of the Census, *Thirteenth Census of the United States 1910*, Vol. I "Population" (Washington: Government Printing Office, 1913), p. 1005.

13 Bureau of the Census, *Fifteenth Census of the United States 1930*, *op. cit., pp. 355–56*.

14 James H. Tashjian, *The Armenians of the United States and Canada* (Boston: Hairenik Press, 1947), pp. 20–25.

15 Bureau of the Census, *Fifteenth Census of the United States*, *op. cit.*, p. 360.

16 Tashjian, *op. cit.*, pp. 20–25.

Chapter 2

1 *25 Years of Progress* (Detroit: St. John Armenian Church, 1956), p. 42.

2 *Detroit News*, September 9, 1896.

3 *Detroit Northside Gazette*, August 18, 1900.

4 During interviews with various Detroit area Armenians, I asked some of them about Dr. Kalaijian. Many had heard about her but only as Mrs. Attarian had ever met her.

5 *Detroit News*, September 6, 1896.

6 Albert Mayer, *A Study of the Foreign Born Population of Detroit 1870–1950* (Detroit: Wayne University Department of Sociology and Anthropology, 1951), p. 36.

7 Bureau of the Census, *Thirteenth Census of the United States 1910*, Vol. I, "Population" (Washington: Government Printing Office, 1913), p. 1014.

8 Bureau of the Census, *Fourteenth Census of the United States 1920*, Vol. II, "Population" (Washington: Government Printing Office, 1922), p. 1016.

9 Bureau of the Census, *Fifteenth Census of the United States 1930*, Vol. III, "Population" (Washington: Government Printing Office, 1932), p. 1155.

10 *Ibid.*, p. 1158.

11 The lowest figure was given by the Rev. Arnak Kasparian, the high figure by many of the people I interviewed.

12 Statement made by Nahabed Aprahamian, personal interview, May 18, 1958. Hereafter cited as Aprahamian.

13 H. B. Boghosian, *Highlights in Armenian History* (Pasadena: Dr. H. B. Boghosian, 1957), p. 147.

14 The 1920 Census figures show 5,025 foreign born Armenian males compared with 1,251 Armenian females for the East North Central States. This four to one ratio of male to female was the highest of any area of the country at the time: New England had 8,624 males compared with 3,835 females; the Middle Atlantic States had 7,165 males compared with 3,747 females; and the Pacific States (California) had 3,917 males compared with 2,471 females. *Fourteenth Census of the United States 1920, op. cit.* By 1930 there was a marked improvement, especially in the East North Central States which had 6,199 males and 3,750 females. *Fifteenth Census of the United States 1930, op. cit.*

15 Statement by Mr. John Bahlavooni, personal interview, March 18, 1958. Hereafter cited as Bahlavooni.

16 Statement by Mr. Kopernik Tandourjian, personal interview, April 16, 1958. Hereafter cited as Tandourjian.

17 Bahlavooni. Mr. Bahlavooni organized the Hunchaks in Detroit soon after he arrived in the city. Mr. Bahlavooni's older brother had been one of the five men who helped organize the A. R. F.

18 *Ibid.*

19 *Ibid.* Mr. Bahlavooni says that the city bred Armenians who came to Detroit after 1908 lowered the standard of conduct in the Armenian community as some among them drank and gambled and misbehaved in other ways. Previous to their coming, the Armenians of Detroit were a very quiet and ex-

tremely well behaved group. Unfortunately Mr. Bahlavooni is one of the few Armenians left who came here prior to 1908.

20   The highest estimate of married couples before 1913 made by a number of the people interviewed was always less than thirty.

21   Some years later, in 1925, some Armenian wives of the Delray community, already angered by the drinking and gambling going on in a few coffee houses, were outraged when one coffee house hired dancing girls. They circulated a petition and finally won their way when it was discovered the coffee house did not have adequate toilet facilities. Thus the coffee houses remained strictly male territory. Bahlavooni.

22   Aprahamian.

23   Aprahamian, October 6, 1957. Statement by Mr. Peter Manoogian, personal interview, December 16, 1957. Hereafter cited as Manoogian.

24   Aprahamian.

25   Aprahamian. Statement by Mr. Melkon Manoukian, personal interview, May 18, 1958. Mr. Manoukian is the son of the chef. Hereafter cited as Manoukian.

26   Aprahamian, Manoukian.

27   Manoukian. Mr. Manoukian has had seven businesses of various types at seven different locations on S. Solvay since 1921.

28   When asked for their estimate of the Delray Armenian community at its height, the people interviewed usually said 3,000. I have checked through Polk's *City Directories* for many of the years between 1900 and 1946 and, by counting Armenian names of occupants for the addresses on the various streets, get a very low figure (about 100) which must be wrong because this includes businesses and residences. For lack of bet-

ter information, I used the number 2,000, which should take into account inadvertent exaggeration.

29 Manoukian. Mr. Manoukian's father was one of the owners of the above-mentioned restaurant.

30 R. T. La Piere "Type-Rationalizations of Group Antipathy; Armenians in Fresno County, California, "*Social Forces*, XV (December, 1936), 234.

31 Manoukian. Mr. Manoukian still runs a variety store on S. Solvay. Every Christmas he holds a Christmas party for the children in the neighborhood, giving each child a present.

32 I visited the coffee house and talked with some of the customers.

33 Bahlavooni. Mr. Bahlavooni worked at Ford in 1907.

34 Aprahamian.

35 Manoogian.

36 Tandourjian.

37 *Ibid.*

38 Sarkis Atamian, *The Armenian Community* (New York: Philosophical Library, 1955), p. 403.

39 Charles A. Vertanes, "The Case of the Cholakian Family," *Armenian Affairs*, I (1949–50), 37.

40 Statement by Mr. George Kanzanagian, personal interview, May 3, 1958. Hereafter cited as Kanzanagian.

Chapter 3

1 The 1930 Census shows that of the 46,561 immigrants speaking Armenian, only 5,180 were in rural areas and of these, 2,970 were in rural farm areas. California had 2,504 living in rural farm areas, and 1,046 in rural non-farm areas. Michigan had 51 and 102 respectively in these same designated areas. Bureau of the Census, *Fifteenth Census of the United*

States 1930, Vol. II "Population" (Washington: Government Printing Office, 1932), pp. 370–74.

2   Aprahamian. Statement by Mesrob Kurajian, personal interview, November 29, 1957. Hereafter cited a Kurajian.

3   Aprahamian.

4   *Ibid.*

5   Manoukian.

6   Federal Writers Project, *The Armenians in Massachusetts* (Boston: The Armenian Historical Association, 1937), p. 36.

7   *Michigan Gazatter* (Detroit: R. L. Polk Co., 1909), p. 3061.

8   Manoogian. Mr. Manoogian was one of the five Armenians on Manchester.

9   Probably more since I counted Armenian names and some Armenians shortened or anglicized their names.

10 R. L. Polk Co., *Detroit City Directory 1921* (Detroit: R. L. Polk Co., 1921), pp. 3023–25.

11 R. L. Polk Co., *Detroit City Directory 1928–29* (Detroit: R. L. Polk Co., 1929), pp. 1228–29.

12 R. L. Polk Co., *Detroit City Directory 1940* (Detroit: R. L. Polk Co., 1940), pp. 3273–75.

13 Most Armenians in Detroit are of peasant or small village background. It would seem that they would have had little opportunity to learn the trade until they reached the United States. The Armenian shoemakers I know had little or no shoemaking experience before going into the business.

14 Letter from Mr. Albert Varoujian, December 7, 1957.

15 Aprahamian. Mr. N. Aprahamian has been in the grocery business for thirty-five years.

16 Statement by Mr. Harry Berberian, personal interview, June 17, 1958. Hereafter cited as Berberian. Mr. Berberian writes a million dollars worth of insurance a year and much of his

business is conducted within the Armenian community of Detroit. His knowledge and estimates of the number of Armenians engaged in business, as well as the types of business or profession, are, to my knowledge, the best available. It is impossible to use a city directory because the owner of a store is rarely listed.

17 *Ibid*. I have talked to several cleaners and they hold this estimate to be conservative.

18 Statement by Mr. Jack Hagop Mooradian, personal interview, June 10, 1958. Hereafter cited as Mooradian.

19 *Ibid*.

20 Statement by M. Selvian, personal interview, July 18, 1958. Mr. Selvian has been a hotel operator for many years.

21 Berberian. The two largest firms are Masco Screw and the Mardigian Corporation.

22 Statement by Dr. N. Kassabian, personal interview, May 24, 1958. Hereafter cited as Kassabian. Statement by Dr. G. Attarian, personal interview, June 29, 1958. Both of these men had their pre-professional training in Armenia, then came to the United States. Dr. Kassabian attended Northwestern University, while Dr. Attarian attended the University of Michigan.

23 Berberian.

24 W. Lloyd Warner and Leo Srole, *The Social Systems of American Ethnic Groups* (New Haven: Yale University Press, 1945), p. 62.

25 *Ibid*., pp.99–100.

Chapter 4

1 Letter from Mr. Albert Varoujan, December 7, 1957. Hereafter cited as Varoujan. Mr. Varoujan was a charter member of the Ramgavar Detroit Chapter.

2 Tandourjian. Mr. Tandourjian has been a field worker for the A. R. F. for many years.

3 Mooradian.

4 *Ibid.*

5 Bahlavooni.

6 Varoujan.

7 Kurajian.

8 Kassabian.

9 Kurajian.

Chapter 5

1 Kurajian.

2 Kassabian.

3 *The Armenian General Benevolent Union Story* (New York: Armenian General Benevolent Union of America, Inc., 1955), p. 4.

4 *Ibid.*, pp. 4–5.

5 *Ibid.*, p. 6.

6 *Ibid.*, pp. 7–9.

7 *Ibid.*, p. 10.

8 *Ibid.*, p. 1.

9 Statement by Mr. Howard Atesian, personal interview, June 19, 1958. Hereafter cited as Atesian.

10 *Ibid.*, Mr. Atesian is a long time member of the Detroit chapter and is at present the president of the chapter.

11 Mooradian.

12 Statement by Mr. Armen Ovhanesian, personal interview, June 26, 1958. Hereafter cited as Ovhanesian.

13 Kanzanagian. Mr. Kanzanagian is secretary for many of these organizations and corresponds with nearly every Armenian organization in Detroit. He consulted his voluminous records

while giving me the desired information. Mr. Kanzanagian, who is retired, is engaged in writing in great detail his personal reminiscences from the day he came to Detroit.

Chapter 6

1 This is practically the same group of men who founded a Congregational Church about this same time. See Chapter 8.
2 Kanzanagian.
3 Aprahamian.
4 Ovhanesian. Mr. Ovhanesian is the president of the Detroit Armenian Cultural Society.

Chapter 7

1 Statement by Mrs. Garabed Attarian, personal interview, June 29, 1958. Mrs. Attarian was very active player and especially helped the touring professional Armenian actors. On occasion she even went to Chicago to help put on a play.
2 Mooradian. Mr. Mooradian was not in Detroit in 1918, but he consulted some records he has in his possession as well as consulting older members of the A. R. F. player group in order to give accurate information.
3 Statement by Mr. Shirinian, personal interview, May 28, 1958. Hereafter cited as Shirinian. Mr. Shirinian headed the A. D. L. player group for many years.
4 Shirinian. Mooradian.
5 Mooradian.
6 Statement by Mr. Harry Ekizian, personal interview, June 15, 1958. Hereafter cited as Ekizian. Shirinian.
7 Shirinian. Mooradian.
8 *Ibid.*
9 *Ibid.*

Notes

10 Shirinian.

11 *Ibid.*

12 *Ibid.*

13 Mooradian.

14 Shirinian.

15 Ekizian.

Chapter 8

1 M. V. Malcom, *The Armenians in America* (Boston: The Pilgrim Press, 1919), p. 17.

2 *Ibid.*

3 Statement by The Rev. Joseph Kalajian, personal interview, May 17, 1958. Hereafter cited as Kalajian.

4 *Ibid.*

5 *The Detroit News*, June 7, 1958.

6 Kalajian.

7 *Ibid.*

8 *Ibid.*

9 *Ibid.*

10 Leon Arpee, *A Century of Armenian Protestantism 1846–1946* (New York: The Armenian Missionary Association of America, Inc., 1946), p. 5.

11 *Ibid.*, pp. 23–29.

12 *Ibid.*, p. 36.

13 Statement by the Rev. Edward Tovmassian, personal interview, April 29, 1958. Hereafter cited as Tovmassian.

14 *Ibid.* Evangelical and Congregational are almost interchangeable terms as far as the Armenian Protestant Churches are concerned since there is only one Presbyterian Church on the eastern states section.

15 Arpee, *A Century of Armenian Protestantism, op. cit.*, p. 96.

16 Kanzanagian.

17 Armenian Congregational Church, "Dedication Program" (Detroit, 1952), p. 2.

18 *Ibid.*

19 Kassabian.

20 Armenian Congregational Church, *op. cit.*, p. 2.

21 *The Detroit Free Press*, September 30, 1927.

22 Undated newspaper clipping in Burton Historical Collection. The Rev. Tovmassian says the price was approximately $40,000.

23 Armenian Congregational Church, *op. cit.,* p. 3.

24 Tovmassian.

25 There are at least two very small splinter groups of Armenians who have organized, after a fashion, their own churches. One is located on Thomson Avenue in Highland Park, the other in a store building on Lafayette, east of Livernois. The latter has the name of the Armenian Evangelical Church. It has no connection with the Armenian Congregational Church according to The Rev. Tovmassian.

26 Rev. Shnork Vartapet Kaloustian, *An Outline of the History of the Armenian Church* (New York: Diocese of the Armenian Church of North America, 1953), p. 7.

27 Bahlavooni. Mr. Bahlavooni served as a deacon in that church service.

28 There has long been close cooperation between the Episcopal Church or Anglican Church and the Armenian Apostolic Church. Though the Orthodox and Catholic Churches are in closer agreement on doctrine with the Armenian Church, there is no close contact. Of all the Protestant sects, the Anglican doctrine is closest to the Armenian Apostolic Church. In the absence of Sunday school texts, Armenian Churches

use the texts designed for Episcopal Sunday school classes. The present pastor of St. John Armenian Church, The Rev. Arnak Kasparian, though educated at the Seminary of the Armenian Patriarchal of Jerusalem, also studied for two years at the Episcopalian Seminary in New York City. Statement by The Rev. Arnak Kasparian, personal interview, May 23, 1958.

29 Manoogian. Mr. Manoogian has long been active in the Armenian Church in Detroit. He has generously given of his time, serving in many capacities, and his money, though he is not a wealthy man.

30 Kurajian, November 29, 1957. Mr. Kurajian was long active in church affairs serving in various capacities.

31 *Ibid.*

32 Ekizian.

33 *The Detroit Free Press,* May 26, 1923.

34 "Minutes of the Parish Council of St. John Armenian Church 1929–1951," April 11, 1932, p. 74.

35 *Ibid.,* April 9, 1931, p. 50.

36 *Ibid.,* April 15. 1929, p. 3.

37 Statement by Mr. Archie Yeghissian, personal interview, May 25, 1958. Mr. Yeghissian, is the present chairman of the Parish Council of St. John Armenian Apostolic Church.

38 "Minutes," *op. cit.,* September 26, 1930, p. 31.

39 *Ibid.,* October 30, 1930, p. 32.

40 *Ibid.,* September 26, 1930, p. 31.

41 *Ibid.,* September 27, 1930, p. 31.

42 *Ibid.,* December 12, 1930, p. 36.

43 *Ibid.,* March 8, 1931, p. 49.

44 *Ibid.,* March 19, 1930, p. 50.

45 *Ibid.,* April 30, 1931, pp. 52–53.

46 Mooradian.

47 Manoogian.

48 "Minutes," *op. cit.*, March 28, 1930, p. 19.

49 *Ibid.*, July 27, 1930, p. 27.

50 *Ibid.*, October 31, 1930, p. 32.

51 *Ibid.*, December 5, 1930, p. 35.

52 Kurajian.

53 "Minutes," *op. cit.*, July 8, 1929, p. 6.

54 *Ibid.*, December 5, 1930, p. 35.

55 *The Detroit News*, August 3, 1931.

56 "Minutes," *op. cit.*, January 24, 1933, p. 101.

57 *The Detroit Free Press*, November 23, 1931.

58 "Minutes," *op. cit.*, July 15, 1931m p. 54.

59 *Ibid.*, August 5, 1931, p. 55.

60 *Ibid.*, January 28, 1932, p. 71.

61 "Treasurer's Report of 1932," St. John Armenian Church.

62 Manoogian. Statements by Dr. Garabed Attarian, personal interview, June 29, 1958. "Minutes," *op. cit.*, May 18, 1933, p. 107.

63 "Minutes," *op. cit.*, February 29, 1932, p. 72 and January 1, 1933, p. 83.

64 *Ibid.*, August 17, 1933, p. 111.

65 *Ibid.*, September 28, 1933, p. 115.

66 *New York Times*, December 25, 1933.

67 *Ibid.*, July 13, 1934.

68 *Ibid.*, July 14, 1934.

69 *Ibid.*, April 10, 1935.

70 Sarkis Atamian, *The Armenian Community* (New York: Philosophical Library, 1955), pp. 92–93. Statement by Antranig Antreassian, personal interview, June 20, 1958. Hereafter cited as Antreassian. Mr. Antreassian is the editor

of *Baikar*, the Armenian language daily newspaper of the A. D. L. party.

71 Atamian, *op. cit.*, pp. 93–94.

72 William L. Langer, *The Diplomacy of Imperialism 1890–1902*, Vol. I (New York: Alfred A. Knopf, 1935), p. 156.

73 *Ibid.*, pp. 156–57.

74 *Ibid.*, p. 157.

75 Federal Writers Project, *The Armenians in Massachusetts* (Boston: The American Historical Association, 1937), pp. 46–47.

76 Langer, *op. cit.*, p. 321.

77 Antreassian. Before becoming editor of the A. D. L. 's Armenian language newspaper in Fresno, California, Atamian, in his book *The Armenian Community*, has information that differs from the information given by Mr. Antreassian. Mr. Antreassian read what Atamian wrote on the formation of the Ramgavar Party, which in turn became the A. D. L. party, while I was interviewing him and said that Atamian was in error.

78 *Ibid.*

79 *Ibid.*

80 Langer, *op. cit.*, p. 155.

81 *Ibid.*

82 *Ibid.*, p. 321.

83 A cipher-telegram from Turkey's War Office sent to all the commanding officers of the army; "February 27, 1916—In view of present circumstances, the Imperial Government has an order for the extermination of the whole Armenian race." J. Messakian, *A Searchlight on the Armenian Question.* (1878–1950) (Boston: Hairenik Publishing Co., 1950), p. 51.

84 *Ibid.*, p. 146.

85 *Ibid.*, p. 148.

86 From conversations I have had with Armenians recently arrived from Turkey, conditions for the Armenians, especially outside of Istanbul, are very bad.

87 K. S. Papazian, *Patriotism Perverted* (Boston: Baikar Press, 1934), p. 57.

88 Antreassian.

89 *Ibid.* Mr. Antreassian was a friend of the Archbishop and was present in Holy Cross Armenian Church at the time of Archbishop Tourian's assassination.

90 *Ibid.*

91 Atamian, *op cit.*, pp. 381–386. Mr. Atamian's work is an apology for the Dashnaktzoutyoun. He, too, brands all who oppose the A. R. F. as pro-Communist, p. 413.

92 Antreassian.

93 Kasparian.

94 *Ibid.*

95 Antreassian.

96 Reuben Darbinian, "On the Softness of Intellectuals Toward Communism," *Armenian Review*, X, No. 3 (Autumn, 1957), 37.

97 *New York Times*, October 17, 1957.

98 *Ibid.*, October 20, 1957.

99 "Minutes," *op. cit.,* December 29, 1933, p. 121.

100 *Ibid.*, February 4, 1934, p. 126.

101 *Ibid.*, February 18, 1934, p. 135.

102 Kurajian.

103 "Minutes," *op. cit.,* March 15, 1934, p. 141. The texts of the two letters were not included in the minutes.

104 *Ibid.*, March 27, 1934, p. 142.

105 Mooradian.

106 Tandourjian.

107 The present pastor of St. Sarkis is The Rev. Sooren Pa-
pakhian.

108 *The Armenian Church* (Boston: North American Diocese,
May, 1958), p. 8.

109 *Ibid.*

110 See any issue of the monthly A. C. Y. O. A. publication, *The
Armenian Guardian.*

BIBLIOGRAPHY

Primary

Alexanian, Mrs. Nevart. Personal interview, June 6, 1958.

Antreassian, Mr. Antranig. Personal interview, June 20, 1958.

Aprahamian, Mr. Nahabed. Personal interview, May 18, 1958.

The Armenian Church. Boston: North American Diocese, May 1958.

Atesian, Mr. Howard. Personal interview, June 19, 1958.

Attarian, Dr. Garabed. Personal interview, June 29, 1958.

Attarian, Mrs. Garabed. Personal interview, June 29, 1958.

Avedesian, Mr. Krikor. Personal interview, May 18, 1958.

Bahlavooni, Mr. John. Personal interview, March 18, 1958.

Berberian, Mr. Harry. Personal interview, June 13, 1958.

Bureau of the Census. *Fifteenth Census of the United States 1930*. "Population," 3 Vols. Washington: Government Printing Office, 1932.

Bureau of the Census. *Fourteenth Census of the United States Taken in the Year 1910*. Vol. I. "Population." Washington: Government printing Office, 1922.

Bureau of the Census. *Thirteenth Census of the United States Taken in the Year 1910*. Vol. I. "Population." Washington: Government Printing Office, 1913.

Darbinian, Reuben. "On the Softness of Intellectuals Toward Communism." *Armenian Review*, X, No. 3 (1957), 34–39

Ekizian, Mr. Harry. Personal interview, June 15, 1958.

Bibliography

Kalajian, The Rev. Joseph. Personal interview, May 17, 1958.

Kanzanagian, Mr. George. Personal interview, May 3, 1958.

Kasparian, The Rev. Arnak. Personal interview, May 23, 1958.

Kassabian, Dr. Nishan. Personal interview, May 24, 1958.

Krikorian, Mr. Arshag. Personal interview, May 18, 1958.

Krikorian, Mr. Sarkis. Personal interview, June 24, 1958.

Kurajian, Mr. Mesrob. Personal interview, November 29, 1957.

Manoogian, Mr. Peter. Personal interview, December 16, 1957.

"Minutes of the Parish Council of St. John Armenian Church 1929–1951."

Mooradian, Mr. Jack Hagop. Personal interview, June 10, 1958.

Papazian, The Rev. Diran. Personal interview, June 16, 1958.

Shagoian, Mr. Sarkis. Personal interview, June 1, 1958.

Shirinian, Mr. Manoog. Personal interview, May 28, 1958.

Shirinian, Mrs. Manoog. Personal interview, May 28, 1958.

Tandourjian, Mr. Kopernik. Personal interview, April 16, 1958.

Torosian, Mr. Toros. Personal interview, March 18, 1958.

Tovmassian, The Rev. Edward. Personal interview, March 16, 1958.

"Treasurer's Reports of St. John Armenian Church" (1929–1957).

Varoujan, Mr. Albert. Letters December 7, 1957; April 21, 1958.

Yeghissian, Mr. Archie. Personal interview, May 25, 1958.

Zadoian, Mr. Hosrof. Personal interview, December 29, 1957.

Secondary

Armenian Congregational Church. "Dedication Program." Detroit: Armenian Congregational Church, 1952.

The A. G. B. U. Story. New York: The Armenian General Benevolent Union of America, Inc., 1955.

Arpee, Leon. *A Century of Armenian Protestantism 1846–1946.* New York: The Armenian Missionary Association of America, Inc., 1946.

Boghosian, H. B. *Highlights of Armenian History and its Civilization.* Pasadena: H. B. Boghosian, 1957.

De Morgan, Jacques. *History of the Armenian People.* Tr. By Ernest F. Barry. Boston: Hairenik Press.

Federal Writers Project. *The Armenians in Massachusetts.* Boston: The American Historical Association, 1937.

A History of Armenian Christianity. New York: The Armenian Missionary Association of America, Inc., 1946.

Kaloustian, Rev. Shnork Vartabed. *An Outline of the History of the Armenian Church.* New York: The Diocese of the Armenian Church of North America, 1953.

Langer, William L. *The Diplomacy of Imperialism 1890–1902.* Vol. I. New York: Alfred A. Knopf, 1935.

LaPiere, R. T. "Type-Rationalizations of Group Antipathy; Armenians in Fresno County, California." *Social Forces,* XV (1936), 232–37.

Malcom, M. Vartan. *The Armenians in America.* Boston: The Pilgrim Press, 1919.

Mayer, Albert. *A Study of the Foreign Born of Detroit 1870–1950.* Detroit: Wayne University Department of Sociology and Anthropology, 1951.

Missakian, J. *A Searchlight on the Armenian Question 1878–1950.* Boston: Hairenik Publishing Co., 1950.

Papazian, K. S. *Patriotism Perverted.* Boston: Baikar Press, 1934.

Polk, R. L., Co. *Detroit City Directory*. Detroit: R. L. Polk Co., 1901–1957.

Polk, R. L., Co. *Michigan Gazetteer 1909*. Detroit: R. L. Polk Co. 1909.

Sarkissian, A. O. *History of the Armenian Question to 1885*. Urbana: The University of Illinois Press, 1938.

Tashjian, James H. *The Armenians of the United States and Canada*. Boston: Hairenik Press, 1947.

25 Years of Progress. Detroit: St. John Armenian Church, 1956.

Vertanes, Charles A. "The Case of the Cholakian Family," *Armenian Affairs*, I (1949), 35–51.

Warner, W. Lloyd. *The Social Systems of American Ethnic Groups*. New Haven: Yale University Press, 1945.

Yeghisheh, Vardapet. *The Epic of St. Vardan the Brave*. Translated by C. F. Neuman, with a commentary and annotations by Vahan M. Kurkjian, New York: Diocese of the Armenian Church in North America.